The Language of Leadership

The Language of Leadership

Roger Soder

Foreword by John I. Goodlad

JOSSEY-BASS
A Wiley Company
San Francisco

Published by

JOSSEY-BASS
A Wiley Company
350 Sansome St.
San Francisco, CA 94104-1

www.josseybass.com

Credits continue on page 211.

Jossey-Bass books and products are available through most bookstores.
To contact Jossey-Bass directly, call (888) 378-2537, fax to (800) 605-2665,
or visit our website at www.josseybass.com.

Substantial discounts on bulk quantities of Jossey-Bass books are available
to corporations, professional associations, and other organizations. For details
and discount information, contact the special sales department at Jossey-Bass.

We at Jossey-Bass strive to use the most environmentally sensitive paper stocks
available to us. Our publications are printed on acid-free recycled stock whenever
possible, and our paper always meets or exceeds minimum GPO and EPA requirements.

Library of Congress Cataloging-in-Publication Data
Soder, Roger, 1943-
  The language of leadership / Roger Soder.— 1st ed.
    p. cm.
Includes bibliographical references and index.
  ISBN 0-7879-4360-6
  1. Leadership.   2. Persuasion (Psychology)   3. Reconciliation.
I. Title.
  HM1261 .S63 2001
  303.3'4—dc21
                                                              2001002464

FIRST EDITION
HB Printing   10 9 8 7 6 5 4 3 2

Contents

Foreword

Readers will realize, only a short way into Roger Soder's Preface, that his book is not an angel food cake recipe for effective leadership. Business executives should expect no lists of things to do in order to keep clients from leaving by the back door while they are ushering new ones through the front. School principals will look in vain for five easy steps to good relationships with parents. Nevertheless, this is an eminently practical book, a handbook for survival as well as excellence in leadership and sleeping with a clear conscience.

Leadership ranks almost with politics and religion as a topic of human interest and conversation. A steady stream of announcements of seminars, new books, and speakers coming to town is directed particularly to the business and educational communities. The common appeal is to individual potential and accompanying financial rewards, power, and prestige. The language of persuasion frequently verges on the spiritual or psychoanalytic. Little is said of the common good. Soder's approach is quite different.

Roger Soder is not, of course, a lone explorer of the high ground of moral leadership. Nor is he naive in assuming that moral purpose provides the leader with a shield against reproach or attack. He does, however, position his message in a context of leadership responsibility that extends far beyond personal aggrandizement. What must the leader know and be able to do in order to advance the cause for which he or she has assumed leadership? There are some parallels here between Soder's analysis of the informational and political context and that of Harlan Cleveland in *The Knowledge Executive*.[1] One needs not only a continuous flow of relevant information but also knowledge of from whence (or whom) it comes. There are clear connections, too, between Roger Soder's concept of moral agency and John Gardner's vision of the leadership needs of civil societies.[2]

Christopher Hodgkinson has written that leadership is essentially a philosophical activity, and "the art of administration finds its true ground in the humanities."[3] Although Soder's uses of "the shrewd observations of others" are not exclusively from scholars in the humanities, they illuminate human paradigms, which in turn illuminate the challenges and quandaries of leadership. If you are not so convinced after reading the first three chapters, read on. The guiding paradigm for getting into things does not necessarily serve one well for the often more difficult task of getting out of them. Knowing one's self may be as helpful as knowing the terrain, and maybe more helpful. The manual detailing seven steps to excellence in leadership might not help at all. Leadership has more to do with ecological relationships than with linear processes, as Soder reminds us, usually with subtlety, more than once.

The popular interest in leadership tends to fasten all too frequently on how to do "it." Some good research on effective schools produced the conclusion that the leadership of principals played a major role. Suddenly there appeared treatises and consultants offering tips to becoming a good principal, some couched in language similar to that of health programs for losing weight. The need to learn more and do more about educating educators to be effective school leaders was reduced not at all.

In Chapter Four, Roger Soder refers to work in which he, colleagues, and I have been engaged over a number of years. Our agenda is daunting: supporting schools and their stewards, who in turn support the enculturation of the young into a political and social democracy. We recognized early the role of leaders, the breadth and depth of their needed leadership, and the moral compass of their charge. A leadership development program has been at the core of nearly all of our ongoing initiatives and has proved to be the most powerful force in advancing the agenda.

Naturally we turned to the literature on educational change and leadership. The work of the late sociologist Paul Lazarsfeld, of Columbia University, attracted our attention. As with our approach, he had created a new setting for advancing a cause and soon focused on the role of leaders in human enterprises. He and his students gathered data on leaders down through the centuries—of principalities, governments, armies, vineyards, shipping companies, monasteries, universities, and more—searching for those generic qualities that surely all leaders must possess. One stood out: successful leaders *worry* about everything—not worry in the sense of being continuously stressed out, although stress has its place. Rather, leaders develop a conceptual span of control that encompasses the major elements of their responsibility and its ecological context. They delegate the handling of details while paying keen attention to this handling. Delegation does not remove the leader from responsibility or the devil from the details. There is a kind of symmetry in this concept, and it is this, I think, more than anything else, that Soder captures in what follows.

A large proportion of treatises on leadership strike me as being out of breath, in a race to be first with the newest in what works. The emphasis is on actions to be taken and outcomes to be realized. Ironically, most of the work of leadership has been accomplished before any overt acts occur. Acclaim for the leader addresses the battle won when it is the wisdom and thoroughness of the planning that warrants applause—planning that includes the management of alternative scenarios.

The bibliographies of treatises on leadership are highly revealing. In the breathless variety, the references are recent. Apparently the new grows old very quickly, and so we are deprived of past wisdom.

How refreshing it is to be reminded by Soder's notes and quotations that wisdom ages well. For graduates of the liberal arts college, a fast-disappearing institution, *The Language of Leadership* will be a refresher and more. For others not so fortunate, the book will be an intellectual feast, a course in itself. For both, there will be wonderment over the perfect match of Roger Soder's point and the precisely chosen quotation to illustrate it. And so pull up a comfortable chair and join in a conversation that has come up through the ages. You might want to dress for the occasion.

Seattle, Washington   JOHN I. GOODLAD
May 2001

Preface

This book is about leadership. It does not attempt to cover all aspects of what it might mean to be a leader. Rather, I dwell on selected elements: persuasion; the creation of a more thoughtful public and the ethics of persuasion; principles, strategies, and costs of information seeking; and, when things go wrong, the leader's role in reconciliation and reconstitution.

Missing here are some of the elements of leadership one might expect. There is, for instance, nothing here that tells leaders how to develop mission statements or strategic plans, nothing on finance or cost control. There is nothing here that bears directly on sales, although as any salesperson will tell you, sales is nothing more or less than persuasion, so in that sense, making the sale is a large chunk of what this book is about.

My approach here eschews most of the usual sources and citations in support of arguments and claims. For the most part, I rely heavily on what I believe to be the shrewd observations of others (along with some modest observations and experiences of my own). Those shrewd observations come to us from across time. Thus, Tacitus observes how people behave after the death of one leader and before the accession of the next: "They must show neither satisfaction at the death of an emperor, nor gloom at the accession of another: so their features were carefully arranged in a blend of tears and smiles, mourning and flattery."

Those shrewd observations can come to us sometimes from soci-
ologists, but they are more likely to stem from the sharp sense of the
superb novelist. Here is Stendhal in *Lucien Leuwen:* "To please her
husband and her party Mme de Puylaurens went to church two or
three times a day; but the moment she entered it the temple of the
Lord became a drawing-room." And in our own time, novelist
Anthony Powell: "He read my thoughts, as people do when their
intuition is sharpened by intensity of interest excited by discussing
themselves."

Already the reader may note a tendency to quote. My intent
here follows Montaigne, and rather than paraphrase, I give his own
justification: "I do not speak the minds of others except to speak my
own mind better." Anyway, how could I begin to paraphrase someone else's good writing? If it serves our purpose to have it at all, we
might as well have it in good form. Take the stunning Wallace
Stevens line from "Thirteen Ways of Looking at a Blackbird": "It
was evening all afternoon." I would not be doing any favors by
rephrasing this as, "During most of the afternoon, the sky was as
dark as it might be during what we call night proper," or "During
the afternoon, it seemed like the evening usually does."

There is more to this matter of quotations than trying to speak
my own mind better. I want to point readers elsewhere, to the good
work and astonishing insights of others over the centuries. I want
readers to talk to these other people over time, across cultures and
nations, in the same way that Plutarch says that he started writing
his *Lives* for others but now continues for his own pleasure: "It is
as though I could talk with the subjects of my *Lives* and enjoy their
company every day." As with Machiavelli fourteen hundred years
on. Machiavelli recounts how he spends his days in exile, going to
town, observing people's behavior—what else—and then in the
evening, he washes up, puts on "garments regal and courtly; and
reclothed appropriately," he goes to his study and his books: "I
enter the ancient courts of ancient men, where, received by them

with affection, I feed on that food which only is mine and which I was born for, where I am not ashamed to speak with them and to ask them the reason for their actions; and they in their kindness answer me."

It will be noted, too, that with the emphasis on observations across time, culture, and nations, I am assuming that human nature has not changed very much. What Thucydides has to say about what people do in times of stress holds as well now as it did some twenty-five hundred years ago.

Readers will note that in much of the book (other than Chapter Five), I seem to be focusing on the less edifying aspects of human behavior. I believe leaders must attend to these aspects for the same reasons people have given for climbing mountains: because they are there. But there is a difference. Mountains can be climbed, or you can decide to view them from afar or ignore them altogether. Leaders, I believe, do not have that choice. People can be good, gentle, kind, loving, forgiving, and amiable. But they can also be nasty, ambitious, sneaky, irrational, selfish, duplicitous, and mean. Leaders might want to believe the positive (as indeed do I), but they will not be doing anyone, including themselves, any favors by pretending that all is sweetness and light, by refusing to attend to the negative parts of human nature.

Overview of the Contents

The book deals with elements of leadership as applied to those in elected and other public offices—those in schools, such as principals and superintendents, as well as those in higher education—and those in the private sector.

Chapter One introduces the major premise that persuasion is a critical part of leadership. If you cannot persuade others of the rightness of your proposals and your view of what needs to happen, you will not be an effective leader. The chapter examines a variety of kinds of persuasion in speech, literature, the arts, and commerce, and distinctions are made between persuasion and nonpersuasion (force and threats of force).

In order to persuade, the leader must construct arguments. Arguments, in turn, must be based on information of one kind or another, and information must be sought before it can be used. Chapter Two presents a detailed examination of five information-seeking principles, along with basic strategies. The chapter continues with a discussion of four aspects of information-seeking costs, with a focus on desired and undesired exchange relationships, and concludes with a consideration of what strategies to follow and what to avoid—and there are indeed pitfalls and traps to avoid.

Information is not sufficient to construct a persuasive argument. A leader must choose from a variety of ways to organize material and to argue. Chapter Three provides a discussion of four basic kinds of argument—from definition, from similitude, from consequence, and from circumstance—and also examines such topics as choice of facts to emphasize, sentence structure, euphemism, and delivery. The chapter then presents a discussion of the ethics of persuasion (an ethical matter because the leader has to choose from different available kinds of argument) and concludes with an analysis of the connection between how one chooses to talk and the larger political and social environment—the ecology of persuasion. The argument here is that unethical ways of talking are not isolated; they are connected to the larger social environment, and when your own discourse is bad, it negatively affects the larger society as well as yourself.

Leadership and persuasion do not take place in isolation. They take place in a political context. Chapter Four contrasts two different and opposed political contexts—despotism and democracy— and shows how citizen behavior, and therefore the behavior of leaders, differs between the two. The chapter then discusses the difference between a persuaded audience and a thoughtful public, and shows how a thoughtful public can survive only in a free, democratic society and is in fact a necessary condition of a healthy democ-racy. The chapter concludes with a consideration of eleven addi-tional conditions necessary for a democracy and why these conditions are best taught and made understood through our schools, and it discusses the role of leaders in sustaining good schools. When leaders sustain good schools, they help sustain a free, democratic society—a benefit in itself and a benefit for leaders who need a political context that will encourage innovation, creativity, and exploration.

Despite leaders' best efforts at persuasion and sustaining a thoughtful public, things go wrong between people. Resentment, grudges, feuds, and other unproductive and unhappy behaviors emerge in even the best-run organizations. Chapter Five examines how things fall apart between people and shows, through a presen-tation of large-scale (national) and small-scale (individual) exam-ples, how leaders can help put things back together through a process of reconciliation and reconstitution. Knowing how to lead in perfect situations is useful. Far more useful is knowing how to put things back together after they have fallen apart.

Chapter Six concludes the book with a summary of lessons learned and directions to be taken if leaders are to be effective at persuasion, at creating and sustaining a thoughtful public in a democracy, and putting things back together through reconciliation and reconstitution. The chapter discusses the limits of traditional change strategies, considers the particularly difficult situation of the newly arrived leader (common in an age of high mobility), and con-cludes with advice on what the new leader should and should not do in order to be ethical and effective.

Seattle, Washington   ROGER SODER
May 2001

Acknowledgments

Many people have supported me over the years in helping develop the ideas reflected in this book and in many other ways.

John Goodlad has provided support, guidance (always indirect, subtle, and unassuming), and many observations about leadership. He is a leader I have been privileged to work with over these many years, and a friend. Ken Sirotnik joined John and me with the creation of the Center for Educational Renewal at the University of Washington. As a friend and colleague, Ken continues to provide support, insight, and honest criticism—all welcome, and all greatly appreciated.

There are others, also teachers of mine, who have helped me formulate some of the basic approaches in this book. John Angus Campbell excited and extended my vision of what rhetoric is and does; his contribution is reflected in Chapters One and Three. Close to thirty years ago, I spent many productive hours in conversation with Richard Andrews about information seeking; those conversations stimulated an ongoing interest, causing me to seek more information about the seeking of information. Some of the results are offered in Chapter Two. Close to forty years ago, I had the good fortune to sit in classes with Richard Weaver and Ralph Lerner. Richard Weaver's emphasis on the ethics of rhetoric made sense to me back then and makes sense now; that sense is, I hope, reflected in Chapter Three. Were Weaver still living, I would presume to take some of his time, every now and then, to listen and to learn. Ralph Lerner spoke to me many years ago about politics and political philosophy, and how to be a better reader. Over the decades, he has gladly taught, and I have gladly tried to learn. He continues to be kind to me and generous with his time. I hope in some small way his contribution and support are reflected in Chapter Four. The students in the Danforth principal preparation program at the University of Washington, as well as those who have participated in the Institute for Educational Inquiry's Leadership Program, have taught me much about forgiveness, reconciliation, and reconstitution in their honest efforts to help me become a better teacher. Their efforts are reflected in Chapter Five.

Lesley Iura has provided support for me and this book from the beginning. Her belief in the project and her polite and quietly persistent inquiries about its progress are greatly appreciated.

My wife, Jane, continues to be a major source of support, not only for this project but for all parts of our life together. The way she lives bespeaks leadership of a most profound kind.

What follows stems in part from these and many other people, but in the end, I must take sole responsibility.

R.S.

The Author

Roger Soder is a senior associate at the Center for Educational Renewal, University of Washington, and vice president of the independent Institute for Educational Inquiry. Soder is the editor of *Democracy, Education, and the Schools* (1996, Jossey-Bass) and co-editor with John Goodlad and Kenneth Sirotnik of *The Moral Dimensions of Teaching* and *Places Where Teachers Are Taught* (both 1990, Jossey-Bass). His articles in professional journals center on education, politics, professionalization, and rhetoric. His research interests continue to focus on the ethics and politics of rhetoric, education, and democracy and on the role of the university in a free society. Prior to joining with Goodlad and Sirotnik in creating the Center for Educational Renewal in 1985, Soder was an administrator in the Cape Flattery School District on the Makah Indian Reservation at Neah Bay, Washington, and education director of the Seattle Urban League.

The Language of Leadership

1

Persuasion

A Critical Function of Leadership

When writers in ancient times considered leadership and human affairs, they adverted to the particular importance of persuasive speech. Some suggested that for all of us, the ability to persuade is critical. Thus, Euripides has Hecuba lament:

> Why
> do we make so much of knowledge, struggle so hard
> to get some little skill not worth the effort?
> But persuasion, the only art whose power
> is absolute, worth any price we pay,
> we totally neglect. And so we fail;
> we lose our hopes.[1]

Hecuba gives us two themes that we explore later in this chapter: the importance of persuasion and our apparent willingness to ignore it or distrust it. Hecuba's daughter, Cassandra, sounds a related theme. Cassandra is given a horrible curse. Apollo bestows on her the gift of prophecy, but after she refuses to be his lover, he curses her; henceforth, although she can see the truth, she will be unable to get anyone to believe her. Thus, Cassandra sees the soldiers inside the Trojan Horse, but unable to persuade, she can only watch with excruciating pain the ultimate fall of her city. "Ye shall know the truth and the truth shall make ye free," Christ says, but for Cassandra, and perhaps for most of us, the truth has to be communicated persuasively. Unable to do this, she experiences frustration and despair.

We can find in ancient writings specific reference to the role of persuasion in leadership. Thucydides alerts us to this role. He has Pericles speak of four characteristics of a good leader: the leader must know what good policy is, must be able to expound that policy and make it clear to others, must not be treasonous, and must not be open to bribery.[2] It is the second of these characteristics that concerns us, and we might reasonably argue that the clear expounding is by implication a basic kind of persuasion. Elsewhere Thucydides speaks of Themistokles as having "the ability to expound to others the enterprises he had in hand."[3] Furthermore, Thucydides tells us that Antiphon was "one of the best men of his day in Athens . . . with a head to contrive measures and a tongue to recommend them." Note here that Thucydides sounds a negative note as well: Antiphon's "reputation for craftiness made the people wary of him."[4]

Writers in ancient Rome give further examples. We find Polybius referring to Aratus as "a perfect man of affairs. He was a powerful speaker and a clear thinker and had the faculty of keeping his own counsel. In his power of dealing suavely with political opponents, of attaching friends to himself and forming fresh alliances he was second to none."[5] In his comparison of Demosthenes and Cicero, Plutarch suggests that "it is necessary, indeed, for a political leader to be an able speaker; but it is an ignoble thing for any man to admire and relish the glory of his own eloquence."[6] In *De Oratore*, Cicero refers to "men of action and as orators" and suggests that these are "two careers that are inseparable."[7] Edward Gibbon, certainly an astute observer of Roman times, notes that "the arts of persuasion, so diligently cultivated by the first Caesars, were neglected by the military ignorance and Asiatic pride of their successors."[8]

Such suggestions of persuasion as a critical aspect of leadership are not limited to ancient times. In his letters to his son, Lord Chesterfield adverted many times to the importance of persuasion: without it, "the best head will contrive to very little purpose."[9] Winston Churchill noted of John Adams, "In his judgments he was frequently right, but he lacked the arts of persuasion."[10] Churchill himself demonstrated his persuasive abilities as a leader. Harold Nicolson gives us a telling example, describing the emergence of Churchill as a leader in Parliament on September 26, 1939:

> The effect of Winston's speech was infinitely greater than could be derived from any reading of the text. His delivery was really amazing and he sounded every note from deep preoccupation to flippancy, from resolution to sheer boyishness. . . . In those twenty minutes Churchill had brought himself nearer the post of Prime Minister than he had ever been before. In the Lobbies afterwards even Chamberlainites were saying "We have now found our leader." Old Parliamentary hands confessed that never in their experience had they seen a single speech so change the temper of the House.[11]

During World War II, Churchill's speeches were critical to holding England. C. P. Snow says it well:

> Like most people of my age, I remember—I shall not forget it while I live—the beautiful, cloudless, desperate summer of 1940. One night I was listening with a friend, for we were never far from a radio that June, to one of the grand Churchillian speeches. The accent was odd, to our more modern English ears. It was nothing like the clipped upper-class English which was already fashionable and was to become more so. The style of oratory, like that of Lloyd George, was obsolescent. But we

noticed neither of these things as we listened that night, and other summer nights. For that voice was our hope. It was the voice of will and strength incarnate. It was saying what we wanted to hear said ("We shall never surrender") and what we tried to believe, sometimes against the protests of realism and common sense, would come true. ("We shall fight on unconquerable until the curse of Hitler is lifted from the brows of mankind. We are sure that in the end all will come right.")[12]

Stephen Skowronek argues that President Franklin Pierce "was a failure, yet, his story is instructive. The problem was not that he lacked the power or inclination to do great things but that he completely lost control over the meaning of what he did. His authority as a political leader collapsed in the exercise of his powers. Presidential history is littered with stories like this. As a rule, power has been less a problem for presidents than authority; getting things done, less of a problem than sustaining warrants for actions taken and for accomplishments realized."[13]

A good many other suggestions can be adduced as to the importance of persuasion and the subtlety with which persuasion must at times be effected. In his *Essay on Man,* Alexander Pope tells us:

> Tis not enough your Counsel still be true,
> Blunt truths more Mischief than nice Falsehoods do;
> Men must be taught as if you taught them not;
> And Things unknown propos'd as Things forgot.[14]

An interesting example of Pope's approach can be seen in the response of Chinese scholars to the "new math" brought to China in the 1600s by the Jesuits. Chinese scholars created a myth that the new Western mathematics had in fact evolved out of ancient Chinese ideas. The new ideas, they felt, would be accepted much more quickly if they were seen as a natural outgrowth of earlier accepted methods.[15] More generally, we can argue that persuasion is a cultural matter, drawing on William McNeill's notion of cultural diffusion: "When a group of men encounter a commodity, technique, or idea that seems superior to what they had previously known, they will try to acquire and make their own whatever they perceive to be superior, but only as long as this does not seem to endanger other values they hold dear."[16]

Early on in *Faust*, Goethe delivers a short disquisition on persuasion:

> Unless you feel it, you will never achieve it.
> If it doesn't flow from your soul
> with natural easy power,
> your listeners will not believe it.
> You can sit down and paste phrases together by the hour,
> cook up a little stew from others' feasts;
> you can blow up miserable flames
> from your heap of ashes
> that will amaze children and monkeys—
> if such little triumphs please your taste—
> but you'll never move others, heart to heart,
> unless your speech comes from your own heart.[17]

Moving to America in the nineteenth century, we find an interesting example of yet another approach to persuasion, one that convinced many Americans to make the westward journey. Persuasion here was based on reports of agriculturists'

> naming soils and shrubs and trees and grasses that were already known to them; describing conditions which they had already been wont to overcome; presenting the exact terms of a battle they knew they could win. Always and everywhere that, and that alone, was the unquestionable magnet—the evidence that success with soil

could be won on terms of farm or plantation life as the prospective emigrants knew about; that known reactions of soil to weather would be experienced; that wood with which they were used to working lay ready at hand; that all the old tricks of the trade would work in the new land.[18]

Finally, we can recall one of many versions of the old story about the son's sending his father a letter asking for money. The father's secretary reads the letter in a monotone: "Send me some money right away. I need books and clothes." When the father heard this, he said, "What an insulting way to ask me for money. I won't send him a dime." Later he tells his wife about the letter. She grabs it and reads it in a tender and emotional voice. "Okay, then, that's different," says the father. "Now he's asking like a gentleman. I'll send him the money."

These several examples suggest that persuasion is important both in itself and as a function of leadership, and there is considerable subtlety as to how persuasion is to be effected. Before we can consider the implications of persuasion for leadership, though, we need to reflect a bit on just what persuasion is and what it is not. We need to look at the kinds of persuasion and how they are manifested in the academic disciplines and in literature and the arts.

Kinds of Persuasion

There are many kinds of persuasion, many ways to try to convince others to believe or act in desired ways. One approach is through what Aristotle would term ethos, or character. The persuasion "works" because of the acknowledged and legitimate character of the persuader. Aristotle notes that ethos is established in the course of the speech. Beyond that, it can be argued that the reputation of character preceding a speaker is of considerable importance. A speaker with a reputation for probity and integrity in her research, her professional life, and her personal life will come to the podium with many in the audience much inclined to her point of view even before she utters a word. Similarly, a person with a reputation for shading the truth (as with the previous example of Antiphon's being distrusted because of his reputation for craftiness) might find an audience already disinclined to be persuaded. In this respect, then, ethos or character is in itself a powerful kind of persuasion.

Aristotle also gives us two other basic ways to persuade: logos and pathos. Logos, persuasion based on reason, logic, and "the facts," appeals to the rational mind; the realm of persuasion here is that of the syllogism, definitions, and logical fallacies. Pathos is persuasion based on the appeal to emotions.[19]

There are some who say that one should always appeal to logos and ignore emotional appeals. James Boswell tells us that Samuel Johnson was one of these, but Boswell cannot agree: "Reasonable beings are not solely reasonable. They have fancies which may be pleased, passions which may be roused."[20]

Of the many examples of appeals to emotion, two stand out for me—one ancient, one modern. The ancient appeal is that of Antony inciting the people against Brutus and the other conspirators. At Caesar's funeral, Brutus speaks first. He relies on reason, and in his short and stodgy speech, he lays out the facts to persuade the people that Caesar deserved to die. The people seem content. But then Antony speaks (against the wishes of Cassius, who, much more than Brutus, knows what can happen when an effective orator takes over). Antony relies (as Shakespeare has it) on emotional appeal. He sets up his audience with weeping (he has to pause, overcome with emotion) and heavy irony (Brutus is an honorable man, he says) and continues rousing the passion with his reading of Caesar's will (seventy-five drachmas for every citizen), displaying Caesar's cloak rent with dozens of knife stabs, and, finally, showing the crowd Caesar's bloody body. In the middle of the speech, a plebeian says Antony is speaking with "much reason," but Shakespeare (and the rest of us) knows better. Shakespeare drives home the point even further by bookending the speech just prior to its beginning with the plebeian's saying, "Caesar was a tyrant" and "We are blest Rome is rid of him," and at its conclusion with the respectful audience, now a mob, shouting "most noble Caesar" as they run through the streets intent on mutiny and murder. So stirred up by this speech with "much reason" that when they happen upon Cinna the poet and confuse him with Cinna the conspirator, they murder him all the same: "It is no matter, his name's Cinna."

Another classic example of appeal to emotions occurred near the end of Lizzie Borden's trial. Borden was accused of the brutal hacking to death of her father and stepmother. Her defense attorney concluded his summation in this way: "'To find her guilty, you must believe she is a fiend. *Gentlemen, does she look it?*' They looked, and saw Miss Lizzie with her high, severe collar; her modestly groomed hair; her long, slender hands and her sharp, patrician features; her unmistakable air of being, above all else, a lady. They looked at her, and her advocate had played his strongest card."[21]

Peer pressure can be a kind of persuasion. The behavior of middle school students comes readily to mind, but others can be just as vulnerable to this kind of persuasion. My wife and I were at a baseball game, sitting directly behind four drunken rowdies. To our right was a young couple, a pleasant young man and his companion. After several innings, our pleasant young man became less pleasant as he began to ape the behavior of the rowdies in front of us, persuaded by their behavior.

Bribery is another kind of persuasion. You need a visa; you want to dodge a speeding ticket; you would like a semiprivate table; you do not want to spend hours waiting in line. There are all sorts of situations in all sorts of cultures where a little bribery, a little sweetening of the pot, can persuade others to do what you want. A variation of bribery as persuasion is raising the compensation of an employee you wish to retain but who is being recruited by a competitor. Another form of this kind of persuasion is exchange, or some sort of quid pro quo. I would like your tickets for the baseball game and will persuade you to give them to me in exchange for my helping you figure out how to install a new shower. Lyndon Johnson's quid pro quo tactics employed during his many years in the Senate give us another example: vote for my bill, and you get something in return; do not vote for my bill, and you get something else in return. It is interesting to note that once Johnson left the Senate to become vice president, he found that his power, that is, his power of persuasion, quickly diminished in the Senate. It is difficult to push people around when all of a sudden you no longer are able to dangle membership on choice committees.[22] As Tacitus comments in *The Annals* (Book 13), power is precarious when it is unsupported by its own strength.

Technical skill and expertise can be seen as a kind of persuasion. I was persuaded to have an operation on my knee by a doctor who gave me the plain facts about my torn meniscus. He spent no time appealing to my emotions or attempting to bribe me or placate me. The plain fact of the matter was that I needed surgery, and the plain fact was given to me by a specialist who was arguing from expertise. Another example, this one involving expertise combined with other forms of persuasion, can be gleaned from strategies used in the midst of a Seattle drought some years ago. Weather conditions were such that for the first time in history, strict restrictions were put on the use of water. The strictest restriction was prohibiting any lawn watering, a particularly bothersome stricture for many people in the area used to year-round green lawns. The first kind of persuasion applied was expertise: the water engineers flat out said that no water whatsoever would be available several months hence if people watered their lawns. It was a most compelling kind of persuasion, one that worked. People did not water their lawns. It should be noted that other kinds of persuasion came into play here. The city council established a regulation prohibiting lawn watering—a kind of persuasion by authority. The mayor, a person highly respected in the community, spoke out on several occasions about the necessity of water use curtailment—persuasion by ethos or character.

For most people, these kinds of persuasion fall within an acceptable range. But there are other kinds of persuasion that might be seen as less acceptable. In Chapter 38 of the Book of Job, we and Job hear God speaking out of the whirlwind, thundering, "Who is this that darkeneth counsel by words without knowledge?" God keeps piling on question after question, showing his power and his greater wisdom. "Where wast thou when I laid the foundations of the earth?" is followed in this and the next three chapters by seventy-nine questions. All Job can say, at one point, is, "What shall I answer thee?" and in the end, Job capitulates: "I abhor myself, and repent in dust and ashes." He is "persuaded." But we might want to raise questions about the kind of persuasion used here. There is a suggestion of oppression, perhaps even force. Perhaps in the great grandeur of the Creator's speaking to a humble human being, we might overlook or find positive interpretations of God's approach. But if the same structure of the exchange took place in a staff meeting, what would we think? In the space of a few minutes, a staff person raises a question, and the chief executive officer (CEO) responds with eighty hard-driving pointed questions without waiting for much of an answer. Most of the others in the room would probably think the CEO was making her point and maybe the hapless staff person capitulated in the end, but they would probably feel uncomfortable and would feel that this was not a very good kind of persuasion. Again, we might think of Lyndon Johnson, with his well-known technique of leaning close to (and over) his target, hands on his target's jacket lapels, "persuading" or helping to "reason together."[23]

Perhaps Job is forced to accede; perhaps not. But we do not have to go far in the world to find manifest examples of force used to "persuade." Again, the ancient writers give us the initial distinction. Plato quotes Gorgias as saying that "the art of persuasion was greatly superior to all others, for it subjugated all things not by violence but by willing submission."[24] In *Agricola*, Tacitus gives us his classic and terse conclusion: "*solitudinem faciunt, pacem appellant*" ("They make a desert and call it peace").[25]

Some years later, writing on his travels north to the Hebrides, Samuel Johnson noted that "to hinder insurrection, by driving away the people, and to govern peaceably, by having no subjects, is an expedient that argues no great profundity of politicks. To soften the obdurate, to convince the mistaken, to mollify the resentful, are worthy of a statesman; but it affords a legislator little self-applause to consider, that where there was formerly an insurrection, there is now a wilderness."[26] Close to Johnson, at least in this respect, is Edmund Burke: "The use of force alone is but *temporary*. It may subdue for a moment, but it does not remove the necessity of subduing again; and a nation is not governed which is perpetually to be conquered."[27]

The question we must ask, then, is whether force is persuasion, and if we say it is a kind of persuasion, we still must determine whether we think it is an acceptable kind of persuasion. I would argue that force is not persuasion: force is evidence of a failure to persuade. James Boyd White suggests something similar: "When persuasion fails, the boundaries of the culture are defined."[28] As was once said to me some years ago, "The only alternative to war is persuasion," and force is a kind of war. In talking about commerce, Alfred North Whitehead makes a similar distinction: "Now the intercourse between individuals and between social groups takes one of two forms, force or persuasion. Commerce is the great example of intercourse in the way of persuasion. War, slavery, and governmental compulsion exemplify the reign of force."[29] Similarly, Marcel Mauss speaks of commerce and exchange as a kind of persuasion: "In order to trade, man must first lay down his spear. When that is done he can succeed in exchanging goods and persons not only between clan and clan but between tribe and tribe and nation and nation, and above all between individuals. It is only then that people can create, can satisfy their interests mutually and define them without recourse to arms."[30]

During Hitler's first visit to Italy in June 1934, Mussolini provided a grim example of the juxtaposition of persuasion and force.

Speaking to a large and demonstrative crowd at the Piazza San Marco in Venice, Mussolini, a "gifted orator and unscrupulous demagogue,"[31] claimed that his ultimate goal was the "greatness of the Italian people . . . the patrimony of the whole nation. This patrimony we will defend against every one. We will defend it by persuasion if possible, otherwise with the song of our machine guns."[32]

A contemporary example of force masquerading as persuasion is found in Part I of the film *The Godfather*. Don Corleone "persuades" a Hollywood producer to cast his godson in the producer's movie—by slaying the producer's favorite horse and, as everyone who has seen the movie knows, putting the horse's head in the producer's bed. Don Corleone echoes what we pick up in Part II of *The Godfather*, with the young Corleone saying he will deal with Fannuci, the Black Hand gangster trying to extort money: "Don't worry—I'll make him an offer he can't refuse." The neighborhood learns quite quickly that Corleone's final offer was to murder Fannuci, and it is shortly after the murder that we see the way Corleone "persuades" the slum landlord. I'm a reasonable man, Corleone says. Do me a favor. Ask around the neighborhood: you'll find I know how to return a favor. And, of course, the slum landlord, when faced with "persuasion" of the argument that what happened to Fannuci will necessarily happen to him, capitulates.

Persuasion in the Academic Disciplines

The academic disciplines, especially what are sometimes seen as the "objective" disciplines, can seem straightforward, with a just-the-facts presentation of data. On closer examination, however, it seems that persuasion is deeply involved. Let us examine in brief the persuasive nature of science, mathematics, economics, anthropology, history, and law.

John Campbell, a perceptive analyst of rhetoric and science, gives us a sense of how the science of Darwin and persuasive efforts of Darwin are intertwined:

To claim that Charles Darwin was a "rhetorician" may seem to confuse the provinces of rhetoric and science. Their juxtaposition, however, is not only warranted; it is also inescapable. Even scientific discourse must be persuasive to rescue insight from indifference, misunderstanding, contempt, or rejection. Aristarchus was not believed when he argued that the earth moved around the sun, and although Mendel discovered the laws of inheritance, he failed to convince his scientific peers. To claim that Darwin was a rhetorician, therefore, is not to dismiss his science, but to draw attention to his accommodation of his message to the professional and lay audiences whose support was necessary for its acceptance.[33]

Thus, as Campbell notes, we can "contrast the reassuring inductivist style of *The Origin* with the rapid sequence of topics, inferences, and reflections on strategies of persuasion one finds in Darwin's notebooks. . . . In the notebooks, we see the young Darwin, even before he solved the technical problem of speciation, thinking of ways to solve the problem of persuasive exposition."[34]

Mathematics is often seen as the antithesis of rhetoric and persuasion, with truth a movement from hypothesis to conclusion through a series of logical steps. But as Philip Davis and Reuben Hersh point out, although "in theory, you should be hearing the presentation of those small logical transformations which are to lead inexorably from hypothesis to conclusion," one will undoubtedly hear other phrases, such as " 'It is easy to show that . . .' 'By an obvious generalization . . .', 'a long, but elementary computation, which I leave to the student, will verify that . . .' These phrases are not proof: they are rhetoric in the service of proof." Mathematics, they suggest, is "a form of social interaction where 'proof' is a complex of the formal and the informal, of calculations and casual comments, of convincing argument and appeals to the imagination and the intuition."[35]

Economics might appear to be immune from rhetorical structuring and appeal, but practitioners of the "dismal science," too, have their own persuasive strategies, using models as literary metaphors and choosing a scientistic language that is actually "the economic scientist's metaphysics, morals, and personal convictions."[36] Economist Kenneth Arrow said that in judging competing theories, he used as a criterion "persuasiveness. Does it correspond to our understanding of the economic world? I think it foolish to say that we rely on hard empirical evidence completely."[37]

Anthropologist Renato Rosaldo pointed out that the "kinds of questions about how to represent other forms of life rarely enter into discussions of method in anthropology. It is as if one imagined that photographs told the unadorned real truth without ever noticing how they are constructed—framed and taken from particular angles, at certain distances, and with different depths of field."[38] Similarly, Clifford Geertz talks of "the difficulty of constructing texts ostensibly scientific out of experiences broadly biographical" and concludes that "finding somewhere to stand in a text that is supposed to be at one and the same time an intimate view and a cool assessment is almost as much of a challenge as gaining the view and making the assessment in the first place."[39]

The field or discipline of history has had its share of claims of objectivity while eschewing persuasive elements. Others have recognized the inherent presence of persuasion. Morris Cohen spoke of "the ideal of an imaginative reconstruction of the past which is scientific in its determinations and artistic in its formulation."[40] In *Style in History*, Peter Gay analyzes the style and persuasive elements of four historians—Edward Gibbon, Leopold von Ranke, Thomas Macaulay, and Jacob Burckhardt—and finds that persuasion is a key factor in the work of all four, even Ranke, the founder of "scientific history."[41]

When we read Gibbon's account of how he decided to write *The Decline and Fall of the Roman Empire*, we are reading the third and final version of this "historical" event. David Jordan gives us the three versions:

> In my Journal the place and moment of conception are recorded; the fifteenth of October 1764, in the close of the evening, as I sat musing in the Church of the Zoc-colanti or Franciscan fryars, while they were singing Vespers in the Temple of Jupiter on the ruins of the Capitol.
>
> It was on the fifteen of October, in the gloom of the evening, as I sat musing on the Capitol, while the bare-footed fryars were chanting their litanies in the temple of Jupiter, that I conceived the first thought of my history.
>
> It was Rome, on the fifteenth of October, 1764, as I sat musing amidst the ruins of the Capitol while the bare-footed fryars were singing Vespers in the temple of Jupiter, that the idea of writing the decline and fall of the city first started to my mind.[42]

We can note the care with which he shaped the juxtaposition of the church services to the Roman ruins. What Jordan points out, too, is that "there is nothing in Gibbon's journal about this moment of conception. The journal speaks only of arriving in Rome and has none of the poetry of even the first, tentative version."[43] If history is simply an "objective" science, without a rhetoric, why would Gibbon spend so much time crafting and reshaping his syntax (and his facts) to present his motivation in the best, most persuasive light?

When we think of law, we are less likely to think of claims of an objective science. Surely, and moving beyond the example of Lizzie Borden's defense attorney, the law involves persuasion. In their practice, lawyers seek to establish reasonable proof, persuasive proof, rather than some sort of final, absolute Truth. In the words of James Boyd White,

Law works by a process of argument that places one version of events against another and creates a tension between them (and between the endings appropriate to each); in doing so, it makes our choice of language conscious rather than habitual and creates a moment at which controlled change of language and culture becomes possible. . . . The multiplicity of readings that the law permits is not its weakness but its strength, for it is this that makes room for different voices and gives a purchase by which culture may be modified in response to the demands of circumstance. It is a method at once for recognizing others, for acknowledging ignorance, and for achieving cultural change.[44]

These examples of persuasion in the disciplines could be extended to include illustrations from psychology, theology, political science, literary interpretation, and women's studies,[45] but the point is made with those I have cited here: persuasion is an inherent part of the disciplines, an inherent part of constructing knowledge and viewing the world so as to make it acceptable to others.

Persuasion in Literature and the Arts

As with the disciplines, literature and the arts are deeply engaged in trying to persuade. Again without attempting to be inclusive, let us touch on novels, drama, music, and art.

A novel wishes to tell us something—about characters and their time, or about the author, or about those of us reading it, or all of these. Whether a novel succeeds in persuading us depends in part on how well the author can convince us that he or she has "been there," especially if we have "been there" too. Those who have hung around pool halls will have a pretty good sense of whether Walter Tevis's *The Hustler* is persuasive, that is, believable. Even those who are less familiar with pool halls can get a bit of sense of whether

Tevis has been there or just read about it as research for his novel. Similarly, the novelist's insights into the psychological makeup of her characters will be persuasive if they accord with our own experiences. If the insights contradict our experiences, then the novelist must bring her full powers to bear to persuade us to look at the world in a different way. To the extent we buy the novelist's insights, characterizations, and arguments, we will say that she has written a "good" novel.

Drama affords ample opportunity for persuasion. A performance of *Hamlet* can be persuasive or not, depending on the ability of the actors, their willingness to put energy and focus into the particular performance, and the mood of the audience. There is nothing given here. After a performance, you can come away moved—that is to say, persuaded—or you can come away unmoved and unpersuaded. I have seen a performance of *Hamlet* that left me caring little whether Hamlet lived or died, as long as he got on with it and did whatever he was going to do so I could get home. And I have seen a performance that made me think anew about Hamlet and myself.

Musical performances are notoriously persuasive or unpersuasive. The notes are the same, the piano is tuned at regulation pitch, and the concert hall acoustics are roughly the same from day to day. But the same piece of music, performed by the same artist in the same hall, might one time leave you cold and another time leave you having had an intense emotional and learning experience. One of my piano teachers once told me a story. He was working as an usher at Orchestra Hall in Chicago during a recital by Vladimir Horowitz. Horowitz played, among other pieces, the Chopin "Military" polonaise, an old warhorse played by most aspiring pianists of varying abilities with varying results. But when Horowitz played the first chord of the polonaise, my teacher said he could feel electricity throughout the hall. And when Horowitz began the great rolling arpeggios in the middle section of the piece, the entire audience stood up as one and remained standing until the end. Here, indeed, was a persuasive performance.

In its own way, dance too is persuasive, or it is not. Costumes, choreography, focus, flow, skill—all contribute to moving us or leaving us uncommitted.

We can experience persuasion in art. A painting is capable of getting us to see the world in a new way. Moving, getting us to see, is a kind of persuasion. We are convinced of something through engagement with the painting. On the other hand, if for whatever reason the painting is not persuasive, we simply move on through the gallery.

Sir Arthur Quiller-Couch gives a good summary of my argument so far. "Who does not seek after Persuasion? It is the aim of all the arts, and, I suppose of all exposition of the sciences; nay, of all useful exchange of converse in our daily life. It is what Velasquez attempts in a picture, Euclid in a proposition, the Prime Minister at the Treasury box, the journalist in a leading article, our Vicar in his sermon. Persuasion, as Matthew Arnold once said, is the only true intellectual process."[46]

The Negative Voices of Persuasion

Thus, we have looked at persuasion, kinds of persuasion, and persuasion in the disciplines and in literature and the arts. It seems a persuasive picture, with persuasion pervading all of our efforts. But we must return to Hecuba and her lament. Why do we neglect persuasion, or, beyond that, what accounts for the considerable opposition to persuasion? Again, we begin with the ancient quarrels, then move to our own time.

In ancient times it is Plato who leads the attack on the rhetoricians. In *The Gorgias*, Socrates concedes that "there are two kinds of political oratory, one of them is pandering and base clap-trap; only the other is good, which aims at the edification of the souls of citizens and is always striving to say what is best, whether it be welcome or unwelcome to the ears of the audience." This second kind of orator, of whom Socrates professes to know no examples and asks to have someone of this kind identified for him, will in "any speech or action by which he seeks to influence the souls of men" focus his attention on "bringing righteousness and moderation and every other virtue to birth in the souls of his fellow-citizens, and on removing their opposites, unrighteousness and excess and vice."[47] For whatever reasons, though, Plato seems to have felt that virtually all oratory was of the first sort—venal, calculating, immoral, calculated not to discover truth but to please the masses by whatever means possible.

In *De Oratore*, Cicero notes that Socrates scorned oratory. Socrates "separated the science of wise thinking from that of elegant speaking, though in reality they are closely linked together. . . . This is the source from which has sprung the undoubtedly absurd and unprofitable and reprehensible severance between the tongue and the brain, leading to our having one set of professors to teach us to think and another to teach us to speak."[48]

Cicero, and others, tried to argue that the two should not be separated:

> For eloquence is one of the supreme virtues—although all the virtues are equal and on a par, but nevertheless one has more beauty and distinction in outward appearance than another, as is the case with this faculty, which, after compassing a knowledge of facts, gives verbal expression to the thoughts and purposes of the mind in such a manner as to have the power of driving the hearers forward in any direction in which it has applied its weight; and the stronger this faculty is, the more necessary it is to be combined with integrity and supreme wisdom, and if we bestow fluency of speech on persons devoid of those virtues, we shall not have made orators of them but shall have put weapons into the hands of madmen.[49]

The severance of philosophy and rhetoric that Cicero speaks of continued for close to two thousand years. Thus, in our own time, we note that the comprehensive, eight-volume *Encyclopedia of Philosophy* has no entry for *rhetoric*. We note too that the journal *Philosophy and Rhetoric,* begun in 1968, had for many years just one editor—always a philosopher—and the journal's editorial board was separated with one listing of philosophers and another listing of those in speech, English, and Classics. The editor was a philosopher. Only in 1991 were the boards combined into one listing and joint editors in philosophy and speech/English/Classics appointed.

In modern times, John Dewey weighed in against persuasion, invoking another modernist, Francis Bacon:

> Bacon also brought his charge against the Aristotelian method itself. In its rigorous forms it aimed at demonstration, and in its milder forms at persuasion. But both demonstration and persuasion aim at conquest of mind rather than of nature. Moreover they both assume that some one is already in possession of a truth or a belief, and that the only problem is to convince some one else, or to teach. In contrast, his new method had an exceedingly slight opinion of the amount of truth already existent, and a lively sense of the extent and importance of truths still to be attained. It would be a logic of discovery, not a logic of argumentation, proof, and persuasion. To Bacon, the old logic even at its best was a logic for teaching the already known, and teaching meant indoctrination, discipling. It was an axiom of Aristotle that only that which was already known could be learned, that growth of knowledge consisted of bringing together a universal truth of reason and a particular truth of sense which had previously been noted separately. In any case, learning meant *growth* of knowledge, and growth belongs in the region of becoming, change, and hence is inferior

to *possession* of knowledge in the syllogistic self-revolving manipulation of what was already known—demonstration. In contrast with this point of view, Bacon eloquently proclaimed the superiority of discovery of new facts and truths to the demonstrations of the old.[50]

If persuasion (and, more largely, rhetoric) is seen as solely as inculcation of already-known "truths," then Dewey has a solid argument. What others (beginning with the Sophists) would say in response is that rhetoric in the proper sense is in large part a process of, as Aristotle put it, "discovering the possible means of persuasion in reference to any subject whatever," and that the act of observing (or discovery) is precisely the kind of inquiry Dewey is talking about.[51]

In our own time, many continue to see persuasion at most as a necessary but unpleasant task. The negative images abound. One recent example stands out for me—a car salesman, talking about his approach to an older couple: "Most people think car salesmen have plaid jackets, white shoes, and Elvis hairdos and that they lie. But I talk to customers and find out what's going on and show a little empathy. [The couple in question] were Christian people, so I let them know I attribute my success to a higher power. You need to find that common ground. In the car business, you have to build the rapport before you go for the jugular."[52]

Advertising is often seen as a virulent activity that is the apotheosis of persuasion. In the 1950s, Vance Packard's *The Hidden Persuaders* sounded the tocsin, with scary claims about subliminal messages in print and television ads forcing unwitting consumers to buy products they didn't want, didn't need, and couldn't afford. Perhaps it was part of the culture of the time that Packard's claims seemed plausible; after all, this was the same 1950s culture that spawned films such as *Invasion of the Body Snatchers*, with the basic theme centering on aliens of one kind or another getting us to do their bidding, and books such as William H. Whyte's *The Organization*

Man, with its emphasis on nonthinking conformity, and David Riesman's *The Lonely Crowd,* with its notions of other-directed beings taking their behavioral cues from others rather than from themselves. The theme continues in the 1970s, as exemplified by Robert Heilbroner's attack. Hielbroner thought advertising "the single most value-destroying activity of a business civilization" and spoke of "the extraordinary subversive influence of the relentless effort to persuade people to change their lifeways, not out of any knowledge of, or deeply held convictions about the 'good life,' but merely to sell whatever article or service is being pandered."[53] The theme continues with Michael Schudson's 1984 contribution, *Advertising, the Uneasy Persuasion: Its Dubious Impact on American Society.*[54] The title nicely sums up the book's main argument—an argument that apparently has as much appeal now as it did fifty years ago.

Advertising runs nose to nose with American politics in helping to give persuasion a bad name. Given the thesis of this book, we would expect to find politics intertwined with persuasion. Politics is about leadership, after all, and it is about getting people to see your point of view and act accordingly. At the same time, we can expect to find that when politics and politicians are seen negatively, the primary weapon of politicians at hand—persuasion—will also be seen negatively.[55] There are a few positive and edifying examples of political persuasion. The *Federalist Papers* is probably the greatest persuasive exposition on American government ever written. And we have Lincoln's Gettysburg Address, an elegant and moving reminder of the fundamental grounding of the nation.[56] On the many other hands, we have American political campaigns engaging in "persuasion" of the most scurrilous sort.[57] We all have our favorite or most obnoxious attack ads, and they run the gamut from the little girl plucking daisy petals (1964, attacking Barry Goldwater) to Willie Horton (1988, attacking Michael Dukakis). Every four years, we find ourselves in the midst of yet another seemingly endless presidential campaign where we are again subjected to incessant television ads, with scenes of the candidate hugging diversity archetypes, the alto tones of the female voice-over oozing sincerity, and soft piano music in the background, or—attack time—sharp focus scenes of the carnage resulting from some of the opponent's policies (dead trees, dead whales, dead people) and black-and-white scratchy images of the opponent looking mean or stupid, with the same female voice-over oozing well-modulated shock and faint disgust, and discordant music in the background.

Part of the current negative sense of persuasion seems to stem from perceptions of persuasion as propaganda or brainwashing. Some of these perceptions seem rooted in images of the dictatorships spanning most of the previous century, with masses of people being swayed at rallies at Nuremberg or in Red Square. And some of these perceptions are based on a kind of relativism or postmodern view of truth. With relativism, I can say that truth cannot be known anyway, so why should I presume to tell you what to do or think? We should not want to impose our values on others. My values are not your values, and I do not want to dictate my values to you, which means that in some sort of strange way, all values are equal. (It is curious and ironic that Plato attacks the rhetoricians for being satisfied with "relative" truth as opposed to absolute truth. He attacks them for being relativists. In our own time, the postmodern relativists attack the rhetoricians for claiming "truth." Once again, the rhetoricians do not seem to be able to come out unscathed.)

For a host of reasons, then, some think that persuasion is dirty stuff, beneath us. What is interesting is that we use it all the same. Even in ancient times, even among those who claimed to disdain it, persuasion apparently had its uses. Cicero notes that Socrates was "the person who on the evidence of all men of learning and the verdict of the whole of Greece, owing not only to his wisdom and penetration and charm and subtlety but also to his eloquence and variety and fertility easily came out top of whatever side in a debate he took up."[58]

And in our own time, I have observed that some of the same folks who argue that persuasion is a bad thing spend hundreds of hours in developing with artful craft a funding proposal or research paper clearly intended to persuade. We might think persuasion is beneath us, but when we write a proposal to a foundation or government agency, we take care that our arguments are in good order (including citing at length someone we suspect will be reviewing the proposal) and that the proposal "looks good," with well-chosen illustrations and an easy-to-read typeface. And we include letters of support, again carefully selected again with an eye to whom we think will be reviewing the proposal.

When we put together our vita, we take a great deal of care in explaining what we did in the past, how we did it, and the significance of it. So important is the vita as a persuasive tool that we sometimes seek professional advice. If persuasion were unimportant or beneath us and if our vita speaks for itself (as nothing but bare facts), then why do we take such care?

We use persuasion because we know that despite disclaimers, there is more to the message than straight, rational recitations of facts and logical argument. We know what would happen if in the middle of a major sales pitch we started talking like Hal, the computer in *2001: A Space Odyssey*. We know the difference between reading the transcript of a trial and being in the courtroom hearing hesitations, tones of voice, pauses between question and response, and all the other parts of communication that have persuasive meaning. We know, with Shakespeare, that there can be "speech in their dumbness, language in their very gesture."[59]

Conclusion

It is reasonable to say that we do use persuasion, all of us. Leaders in particular try to persuade. Thucydides is not off the mark in suggesting that persuasion is a critical part of leadership. Is this all leaders do? Clearly no. There are many aspects of leadership. But without the ability to persuade, leaders will have no following. All of the big ideas, mission statements, five-year strategic plans, goals, and objectives will not matter much at all if leaders cannot persuade people that what they are saying makes sense and is worth doing.

What we turn to now is a fundamental part of persuasion: the choice of arguments that the leader will use. Choice of arguments depends on two factors: the kinds of information the leader seeks, obtains, and subsequently chooses to bolster the persuasive case, and the kinds of arguments the leader chooses. We consider these two factors in Chapters Two and Three.

2

Information Seeking
Principles, Strategies, Costs

Why is information seeking such an important part of leadership and persuasion? For our purposes here, three reasons can be adduced. First, the leader must have knowledge of the proper policy, as Pericles reminds us. Knowledge of the proper policy can come only through the seeking of information; only rarely does it come from luck, Ouija boards, or astrology. Second, again following Pericles, the leader must have the ability to expound policy, to persuade others of the rightness of the proposed policy. Here we are talking of *invention*, in terms of classical rhetoric, of discovery of arguments. What are you going to talk about? With what terms and values? What arguments are you going to use? In order to make these choices, one must seek information.

Third, the leader must have a good sense of how people are going to respond to the proposed policy, and that sense can come only from information. As Gregory Bateson notes,

> The man "in power" depends on receiving information all the time from outside. He responds to that information just as much as he "causes" things to happen. It is not possible for Goebbels to control the public opinion of Germany because in order to do so he must have spies or legmen or public opinion polls to tell him what the Germans are thinking. He must then trim what he says

to this information; and then again find out how they
are responding. It is an interaction, and not a lineal situation.[1]

To the extent possible, information should be sought before
making a decision to be able to predict reactions. A leader can get
feedback after a bad policy is enacted and then change that policy,
but after several such policy recisions in the face of negative information, the leader might well be seen as indecisive. Machiavelli
says of the emperor Maximilian, "The things he does on one day he
destroys on another, that no one ever understands what he wants
or plans to do, and that one cannot found oneself on his decision."[2]
On the other hand, the leader who enacts bad policy and then
refuses to change it (not wanting to seem indecisive) runs the risk
of being seen as stubborn and inflexible, defending a bad policy in
order to appear strong.

For reasons of policy determination, persuasion, and feedback,
information is of critical importance. But information seeking is a
complicated business. It is not straightforward; it is not just about
talking to people and getting their honest views, or commissioning
a study, or hiring an evaluation consultant. It is not a matter of getting just the facts. You need to gather information. But you cannot
gather all available information; you do not have the time or the
money, and other people will not necessarily give you all that you
need. You have to choose what information you think you might
want to gather—a difficult task if you lack some sense of what you
are looking for. And you have to choose how you are going to get
the information, and you have to think long and hard about what
that getting is going to cost and what kinds of traps you might have
laid for yourself in the apparently innocent act of asking a question
of someone. And you are going to have to choose what information
to share, because you do not have the time to share everything and
you do not have the legal and the moral authority to share every-

thing. In fact, you will be prevented by legal authority the sharing of everything.

Information seeking is thus fraught with danger; there are mine-fields for the unsuspecting novice and even for the veteran player. The dangers of information seeking were recognized in ancient times, as, for example, in *Oedipus the King*. At the beginning of the play, Sophocles shows us how Oedipus, up to this point a ruler with honor, seeks information from an oracle as to the cause of the plague that has descended on Thebes. The reply from the oracle— the reply that sets everything into motion—is that Thebes must rid itself of pollution. Oedipus seeks further information from Tieresias, the blind seer, who responds, "You yourself are the murderer you seek." When in a rage Oedipus chastises the seer, Tieresias says, "I would not have come either had you not called me." Inexorably, negative information is piled on, from Jocasta, to the messenger, to the herdsman. There are warnings along the way. "I am on the brink of dreadful speech," says the messenger, telling Oedipus not to push ahead. Oedipus does push ahead, of course, and we know the terri-fying outcome.

Two thousand years later, Shakespeare gives us examples of the dangers of information seeking in *Hamlet*. The much too clever Polonius hides behind the curtain in Gertrude's bedroom to spy on young Hamlet. When he lets out a cry for help, thinking that the queen is being attacked, Hamlet runs his sword through the curtain—and through Polonius. Hamlet says to the corpse, "Thou wretched, rash, intruding fool. . . . Thou find'st to be too busy is some danger." Indeed. The costs of information seeking for Polonius were high. Later, Hamlet's erstwhile friends and school-mates, Rosencrantz and Guildenstern, turn spy for the king. They lose Hamlet's friendship, of course, and much more: Hamlet has them killed. Learning of the imminent death of the two spies, Hamlet's true friend, Horatio, expresses shock. Hamlet responds to Horatio with, "Why man, they did make love to this employment. They are not near my conscience, their defeat does by their own insinuation grow."[3] For them too, the costs of seeking information were high.

We might think we can avoid such dramatic and dangerous situations. But at the same time we do have some sense that it is dangerous not to seek information. If you do not get the information you actually need, you won't be able to determine good policy, or make good decisions. You won't have a good sense of how you should talk as you try to persuade others. And you won't be likely to know what people are thinking, what kind of mood they are in, how your proposed policy or decision is going to go over. Sometimes it might appear tempting not to seek information, either because you are confident (perhaps overconfident) or because you simply do not want to hear the bad news. Near the end, as he faces his last battle with confidence, or perhaps overconfidence, Macbeth says, "Bring me no more reports." But in the end, we know that despite all, we need to seek information if we are to function well.

It might be argued that given the dangers of information seeking, a middle ground or strategy might be prudent. The strategy would be not to deny the information that comes your way, but not to go out of your way to seek it. But it is dangerous to remain passive, to let the information just come to you. You will not have any way to verify the information that is brought to you. Furthermore, you have no choice as to the information, its sources, or its reliability. You will have little sense of context, so you will have little understanding of what is given you. You will have given all control over to others and will be nothing but a puppet.

All told, information seeking is a critical part of leadership. From Zen teachings in the tenth- to thirteenth-century Song dynasty we find this advice of Caotang:

> There is nothing special about leadership—essentially it
> is a matter of controlling the evils of biased information
> and autocracy. Do not just go by whatever is said to you
> first—then the obsequities of petty people seeking favor

will not be able to confuse you. After all, the feelings of a group of people are not one, and objective reason is hard to see. You should investigate something to see its benefit or harm, examine whether it is appropriate and suitable or not, then after that you may carry it out.[4]

With the advice of Caotang in mind, let us turn to a brief discussion of basic principles, strategies, and costs of information seeking.

Five Basic Principles of Information Seeking

Of the basic principles of information seeking, five have particular salience, I believe, for the conduct of leadership.

1. Many people will tell you what they think you want to hear.

In the *Laches*, Plato notes that when some people are asked for their opinion, they "will not say what they think. They guess at the wishes of the person who asks them, and answer according to his, and not according to their own, opinion." Plato goes on to say that a condition for taking people into your counsel is that they "will say exactly what [they] think."[5]

Flattery can get in the way of truth. There is an old saying, in many forms, to the effect that friends do not flatter. Tocqueville says as much in the Preface to *Democracy in America*. He is critical of democracy, he says, because he is its friend. In similar manner, Shakespeare's *Julius Caesar* speaks of flattery in this way:

> CASSIUS: You love me not.
> BRUTUS: I do not like your faults.
> CASSIUS: A friendly eye could never see such faults.
> BRUTUS: A flatterer's would not, though they do appear
>   As huge as high Olympus.[6]

Flatters have trouble with the truth. Even more largely, whether we be flatterers or not, there is some question as to the wisdom of telling or not telling the whole truth, the entire truth, and nothing but the truth. Francis Bacon can be called as a witness here, with his observation that "it asketh a strong wit and a strong heart to know when to tell truth, and to do it."[7] A major theme in Molière's *The Misanthrope* is the circumstances under which one should tell the truth, with one character saying under all circumstances, and his friend saying that diplomacy and tact are important, and thus the truth should be shaded. Benjamin Franklin can be called as a witness too, with his admonition to "Use no hurtful Deceit," a notion that suggests at least one kind of deceit that is unhurtful.[8] Lord Chesterfield's maxim applies here: "It is hard to say who is the greatest fool: he who tells the whole truth, or he who tells no truth at all."[9] In *Elmer Gantry*, Sinclair Lewis has one character ask, "Don't you ever tell the truth?" and another respond, "Never carelessly."[10]

What these witnesses suggest is what most of us find ourselves doing. We shade the truth quite commonly, mostly, at the very least, to avoid hurting other people. Someone has bought a new coat or tie and clearly likes the purchase. He ask you for your opinion, and while you think to yourself that the choice is neither good nor bad, you will most likely come out with at least a vaguely positive statement of approval and support.[11]

Machiavelli warns that the courts are full of flatterers and that "men will always turn out bad for you unless they have been made good by a necessity."[12] What that necessity might be varies, of course, with the taste and culture of the leader. One might get people to be good, that is, to tell you the truth, by rewarding them with money, high position, and praise. Or one might try to seek information by nastier means, through bribes combined with threats. An administrator in a school district might want to find out what is going on by using subtle combinations of rewards and implied threats of punishments, such as better assignments, expedited delivery of materials, or participation in a high-status task force that might lead to further advancement. Mata Hari sometimes reappears in strange forms.

There are much nastier ways to seek information: force, terror, and torture, either horribly threatened or horribly real. In *1984*, we cannot help but be sickened by the torture of Winston Smith. By the time the interrogator in Room 101 is done with him, Winston is completely broken, willing to say anything to stop the pain and the threat of the rat about to chew his face.

There are ethical problems here, which we will attend to at the conclusion of this chapter. But what we can say for the moment is that many people will be likely to tell you what they think you want to hear, and the likelihood poses dangers for the leader.

2. People often won't tell you the truth because they don't want to compromise themselves.

In Act V of *Macbeth*, we listen to the exchange between the gentlewoman attending Lady Macbeth and the doctor who has been appointed to look to the health of the queen. The doctor knows of her sleepwalking. Beyond that, he asks, "What, at any time, have you heard her say?"

> GENTLEWOMAN: That, Sir, which I will not report after her.
> DOCTOR: You may, to me; and 'tis most meet you should.
> GENTLEWOMAN: Neither to you nor any one; having no witness to confirm my speech.[13]

With his usual economy, Shakespeare here gives us two reasons for refusing to divulge information. First, the gentlewoman will not pass along information because her mistress told her not to. A demand for information is countered by a higher demand to withhold it, in much the same way that a king will have no success in demanding from a priest information obtained as part of a confession. But there is a second reason for her reticence: having "no witness" to confirm what she might say. Similarly, some people who see crimes committed refuse to divulge information because they do not think anyone will believe them anyway (and, moreover, they might somehow get involved willy-nilly in something they would prefer to avoid in the first place). Other people will not provide information because they do not want to look like fools. It is not all that easy, even if you think your senses have not tricked you, to claim that you have seen a UFO or a susquatch.

3. The power of the leader can get in the way of getting people to tell the truth.

All too often leaders, angry with the perceived negative information given them, shoot the messenger. Macbeth says to a messenger, even before he has heard all the bad news, "Devil damn thee," and calls him "lily-livered" and "villain," and tells him to "take thy face hence."[14]

Francis Bacon, who certainly had enough experience in these matters, tells us that "princes being full of thoughts and prone to suspicions, do not easily admit to familiar intercourse men that are perspicacious and curious, whose minds are always on the watch and never sleep; but choose rather such as are of a quiet and complying disposition, and submit to their will without inquiring further, and shew like persons ignorant and unobserving, and as if asleep; displaying simple obedience rather than fine observation."[15]

Bacon's observations are echoed by Julius Caesar in his observations about Cassius, a threatening man who "looks quite through the deeds of men." Rather, Caesar says,

> Let me have men about me that are fat,
> Sleek-headed men, and such as sleep-a nights.
> Yond Cassius has a lean and hungry look:
> He thinks too much; such men are dangerous.[16]

If leaders are to get the best possible information and advice, they must not surround themselves with flatterers or those of quiet and complying disposition. Rather, leaders must tell messengers and advisers that they will not be angry no matter what is said.

"Zilu asked Confucius how to serve a prince. The Master said: 'Tell him the truth even if it offends him.'"[17] Easy to say, of course. But the leader has to provide support if people are to tell truths, especially unpalatable truths. And as we have seen, Plato argues that if you want to have advisers, a condition for choosing them is that they "will say exactly what [they] think."

In Chapter 23 of *The Prince*, Machiavelli argues that "there is no way to guard oneself from flattery unless men understand that they do not offend you in telling the truth." Near the end of this chapter, Machiavelli returns to this theme: "But he should be a very broad questioner, and then, in regard to the things he asked about, a patient listener to the truth; indeed, he should become angry when he learns that anyone has any hesitation to speak it to him."[18]

During her first day as queen, Elizabeth I hired William Cecil as her first minister, telling him much the same:

> I give you this charge that you shall be of my Privy Council and content to take pains for me and my realm. This judgment I have of you, that you will not be corrupted by any manner of gift and that you will be faithful to the state; and that without respect of my private will you will give me that counsel which you think best; and if you shall know anything necessary to be declared to me of secrecy you shall show it to myself only. And assure yourself I will not fail to keep taciturnity therein and therefore herewith I charge you.[19]

"Without respect of my private will" was a phrase of key importance to Cecil, and one that he apparently took to heart during his decades of service to the queen.

Shooting the messenger has far-reaching consequences beyond the immediate. When a leader gets angry at the messenger, the messenger will be less likely to provide information in the future.

Others in the organization will hear, given the highly developed nature of informal networks. The word spreads rapidly: Did you hear what happened to Ruth when she tried to tell the new principal about the lack of textbooks? She got yelled at by that idiot. No percentage in trying to tell *him* anything.

4. Leaders must be aware of the dangers of optimism and preconceived ideas.

In his *Confessions*, Augustine avers he has "met many who wished to deceive, but not one who wished to be deceived."[20] Some may think that Augustine may have been deceiving himself here. We can adduce all sorts of examples of wishing to be deceived. Someone faced with a serious illness may not want to know just how bad things are; in fact, she might want to be lied to about the danger she is in so she can take some solace in hope ("danger's comforter," Thucydides tells us). Someone has a vague sense that his partner is being unfaithful, in affairs of business or of the heart, but will prefer to deceive himself rather than face the truth and its implications square on.[21]

In the 1500s, Philip II supported the plot to murder Queen Elizabeth and put Mary Stuart on the English throne. He assumed that there would be no resistance to him or to Mary once Elizabeth was dead: "This was a very implausible supposition, but then Philip . . . had little knowledge of the temper of parliament, and he was always fed with wildly optimistic estimates not merely of the numbers of English Catholics, but of their willingness to betray their country. The French, who of course had an embassy in London, were much better informed, and correspondingly less sanguine."[22]

Because of optimism and preconceived ideas, we sometimes avoid seeking information from people who might give us other than what we want to hear. Plutarch says of the conspirators against Caesar, "They concealed the plot from Cicero, though he was very much trusted and as well beloved by them all, lest, by his own disposition, which was naturally timorous, adding now the weariness and caution of old age, by his weighing as he would do, every particular, that he might not make one step without the greatest security, he should blunt the edge of their forwardness and resolution in a business which required all the despatch imaginable."[23]

In *The March of Folly*, Barbara Tuchman addresses situations in which a bad policy is followed, even in the face of clear and negative information about that policy—classic examples of the influence of optimism and preconceived ideas on leaders. The fall of Troy, after bringing into the city the giant horse (and the Greek soldiers), despite Cassandra's warnings is one example; the persistence of British myopia, leading to the loss of their wealthiest colony yet another.[24]

In our own time, we can reflect on Lyndon Johnson, who apparently got to the point that he did not want to see anyone who had anything negative to say about the Vietnam War. Unlike Macbeth, he wanted reports, but only those that supported his position, and he rejected messengers bringing bad news. Thus, when Robert Mac-Namara began to have doubts about the war, he was "gradually eased out of his powerful position, finding himself less and less welcome at the White House, until finally he was removed from his high office."[25]

The preconceptions that can get in the way of seeking and understanding information extend to prejudice and fear. Sometimes we reject information because it comes from a person with relatively low traditional status in an organization, and sometimes we accept information simply because it comes from a high-ranking official or a paid outside consultant. The tendency to act on this kind of prejudice is an old one, as evidenced by this admonition from ancient China: "Useful suggestions should not be rejected just because they come from people in low positions, nor should useless suggestions be followed just because they come from people in high positions. Right and wrong are not a question of social status. Enlightened leaders listen to their ministers: if their plans are useful, the leaders do not look down on them because of rank; and if what they say is feasible, the leaders do not care about how they say it."[26]

From ancient times to our own, good leaders have always had the good sense to seek and sift information with realism and a minimum of preconception and self-deception.

5. How you go about seeking information speaks to your character.

How a leader seeks information has a direct bearing on the leader's legitimacy as a leader. Seeking information always brings into question how you are regarded by others and what kind of information— and support—you will receive.

Machiavelli points out that the prince must be a great seeker of information but a selective seeker as well: "A prince should always take counsel, but when he wants, and not when others want it; he should discourage everyone from counseling him about anything *unless he asks it of them.*" The reason for this strategy, Machiavelli says, is that "there is no other way to guard oneself from flattery unless men understand that they do not offend you in telling the truth; *but when everyone can tell you the truth, they lack reverence for you.*"[27]

This notion of discouraging information flow goes counter to conventional wisdom about open-door policies of leaders. Machiavelli is a most careful and insightful thinker and writer. Some reflection on his advice will show that, as usual, he is on to something here. Not always do we want to let anyone have any kind of input under any set of circumstances, despite our talk about always being open to everyone. There is, for example, the matter of time. If you have a lot of time before having to make a decision, you might want to get lots of input from lots of people. But let us say the river is rising, the flooding is sure to come before midnight, and decisions have to be made about what to do in the next six hours. If the mayor calls for a broadly representative citizens' committee to deliberate, take public testimony, and the like, she will probably be roundly criticized for malfeasance. This may seem like an extreme example. But we can find similar situations in any organization, perhaps less dramatic but applicable nonetheless. On a day-to-day basis, a principal will find that she really does not have the time for the staff member who wants to advise her until the wee hours about what should be done about another teacher. In fact, no matter how much time the principal wants to allot, she probably will not want to spend too much time allowing someone to tell her what and how and why she needs to discipline another teacher. There is a point— almost always a point, I should say—when the staff member must be told, in effect, "Thank you, Mr. Jones, but that's a matter I cannot and will not discuss with you."

We need to remind ourselves that many staff members spend considerable time seeking information as to how their leaders seek information. If you allow everyone to advise you on everything, bringing you every kind of information, data, gossip, calumny, and slander, you will become disrespected. Lord Chesterfield's observation is just as true in our own time as it was in the mid-1700s: "Seem always ignorant (unless to one most intimate friend) of all matters of private scandal and defamation, though you should hear them a thousand times; for the parties affected always look up the receiver to be almost as bad as the thief."[28] Moreover, you will be seen as wasting your time, indulging the office gossip instead of getting to work on sorely needed projects.

Another aspect of character is at work here. There is an ethics of information seeking, just as there is, more largely, an ethics of persuasion on which that information is based. In some instances, the ethics of information seeking seems dated or belongs to a larger ethos not in keeping with our own. In the early days of the British Secret Service, it was a staple that "gentlemen do not read the mail of others." Today, intelligence agencies as well as corporation inquisitors read mail and e-mail with no compunction, and wiretapping is readily justified. But such activities have ethical implications—implications for the character of the leader and for the larger organizational and political context. Some two thousand years ago, Pliny the Younger was representing the Emperor Trajan in Bithynia. He told the emperor of the anonymous pamphlets being circulated, accusing various persons of being Christians. Trajan wrote back, saying that "pamphlets circulated anonymously must play no part in any accusation. They create the worst sort of precedent and are quite out of keeping with the spirit of our age."[29] If you are seen as willing to lie, spy, encourage gossip, and set people against each other, you will lose, and deservedly, the respect of those you profess to lead, as well as the respect of others who will inevitably hear of your ways of seeking information. As we will note in Chapter Three, there is an ecology of ideas and an ecology of rhetoric. There is also an ecology of information seeking, and how you seek information speaks far louder than whatever professions of character you might want to make.

Strategies for Information Seeking

What with all the difficulties of seeking information and the unwillingness of people to provide information and yet their willingness to provide what they think is acceptable (if not necessarily true) information, the leader seeking information will at times have to apply strategies that go beyond the obvious. "There's no art to find the mind's construction in the face," King Duncan tells us just as Macbeth is coming onstage. How right the king was: the man he trusts and rewards ends up murdering him.

If people will not tell you the truth for a host of reasons, then straightforward information-seeking strategies might not be very effective in getting what you need. Other strategies, ones perhaps more devious and less straightforward, have been developed and used over the years, We need to consider these strategies, their effectiveness, and their effects.

One such strategy is to be free with your confidences, thus

encouraging others to be free with theirs. The marquis de Custine relates being treated to this strategy during his journey to Russia in the late 1830s. On the train to St. Peterburg, Custine was approached from time to time by someone who looked like a professor, a Russian scholar, who reports that "he has just traversed Europe and is returning to Russia full of zeal, he says, to propagate there any good that is in the modern ideas of the people of the West. The freedom of his conversation appeared suspicious to me . . . it was a studied liberalism calculated to make others talk."[30]

Another such strategy is to pretend that you do not know what in fact you might know, so that you can allow people the pleasure of correcting your errors. We can observe this strategy in Act II, Scene 1, of *Hamlet*. This is a lengthy and seemingly obscure scene, one usually cut from stage and movie productions because it does not seem to move the action forward very much. The cutting is unfortunate, because the scene gives us, fairly early on, the devious Polonius in full form as the man of the world, the all-knowing and subtle spy, and thus we are prepared for the irony of Polonius's losing his life by being, as Hamlet says of him, a "rash, intruding fool." Polonius wants to know what his son, Laertes, is doing at school. So he intends to send his man, Reynaldo, to spy on his son, telling Reynaldo to avoid direct questions: "By this encompassment and drift of question . . . come you more the nearer than your particular demands will touch it." He goes on to suggest that Reynaldo should "lay slight sullies" on his son, such as, "'I know the gentleman; I saw him yesterday, or t'other day, Or then, or then, with such, or such; and, as you say, There was he gaming; there overtook in his rouse; There falling out at tennis,' or perchance, 'I saw him in a brothel,' or so forth." The information-seeking strategy is subtle and simple: spread some rumors and see whether people confirm or deny what you say:

> Your bait of falsehood takes this carp of truth:
> And thus we do of wisdom and of reach,

> With windlasses and with assays of bias,
> By indirections find directions out.[31]

Lord Chesterfield advocates much the same indirect information-seeking strategy in one of his many letters written to his son in the mid-1700s. This letter is worth quoting at some length:

> It is, for instance, commonly adviseable to seem ignorant of what people offer to tell you; and when they say, Have you not heard of such a thing? to answer, No, and to let them go on; though you know it already. Some have a pleasure in telling it, because they think that they tell it very well, others have a pride in it, as being the sagacious discoverers; and many have a vanity in shewing that they have been, though very undeservedly, trusted: all these would be disappointed, and consequently displeased, if you said Yes. . . . and [when scandal becomes] the topic of conversation, always seem to be a sceptic, though you are really a serious believer; and always take the extenuating part. But all this seeming ignorance should be joined to thorough and extensive private informations; and, indeed, it is the best method of procuring them; for most people have such a vanity in shewing a superiority over others, though but for a moment and in the merest trifles, that they will tell you what they should not, rather than not shew that they can tell what you did not know; besides that such seeming ignorance will make you pass for incurious, and consequently undesigning. . . . Fish judiciously, and not always, nor indeed often, in the shape of direct questions; which always put people on their guard, and often repeated, grow tiresome. But sometimes take the things that you would know for granted; upon which somebody will, kindly and officiously, set you right: sometimes say that

you have heard so and so; and at other times seem to know more than you do, in order to know all that you want: but avoid direct questioning as much as you can.[32]

Lord Chesterfield was seen by some contemporaries as a bit shallow, superficial, calculating, not terribly sincere, and underhanded. (Samuel Johnson said that Chesterfield's letters to his son taught "the morals of a whore and the manners of a dancing master.")[33] What are we to make of these crafty ways of seeking (and withholding) information? We might look askance at his advice to his son, thinking that no one should be so devious. Nonetheless, when we consider the strategy of "seeming ignorance" in the light of our own experience, we might find times when we too have allowed someone to tell us something we already knew because we sensed she would be hurt or miffed if she did not get her chance to shine. Moreover, we usually are cautious about what we say to other people, not necessarily to advance our own interests but sometimes to avoid having other people feel hurt. One does not have to have the cynical views of human nature that Lord Chesterfield evidently harbored to realize that although honesty might be the best policy, prudence is sometimes an even better one.

Francis Bacon gives us several devious information-seeking strategies. He suggests that "because it works better when anything seemeth to be gotten from you by question than if you offer it of yourself, you may lay a bait for a question by showing another visage and countenance than you are wont; to the end to give occasion for the party to ask what the matter is of the change."[34] Bacon also suggests that a "sudden, bold, and unexpected question doth many times surprise a man, and lay him open."[35] (Some readers may recall *Colombo*, a television program from the 1970s in which the hero made a habit of springing odd and unexpected questions on a suspect.) Following a path similar to Polonius and Lord Chesterfield, Bacon finds some virtue in the "good shrewd proverb of the Spaniard, *Tell a lie and find a troth*," although he finds that being too clever by far in such matters can deprive "a man of one of the most principal instruments for action, which is trust and belief." He concludes that the best policy is to have "openness and fame in opinion [that is, a reputation for frankness], secrecy in habit, dissimulation in seasonable use, and a power to feign, if there be no remedy."[36]

So Bacon tells us that truth telling depends on the situation. Be open and frank (or at least be prudent enough to cultivate a reputation for openness and frankness), but be prepared to lie if need be.

Montaigne too suggests that dissembling might be necessary from time to time, but he warns that such behavior will always have negative consequences:

> We must not always say everything, for that would be folly; but what we say must be what we think; otherwise it is wickedness. I do not know what people expect to gain by incessant feigning and dissimulating, unless it is not to be believed even when they speak the truth. That may deceive people once or twice; but to make a profession of covering up, and to boast, as some of our princes have done, that they would throw their shirt in the fire if it were privy to their real intentions . . . and that a man who does not know how to dissemble does not know how to rule—this is warning those who have to deal with them that all that they say is nothing but deceit and lies.[37]

We will have occasion in later chapters to explore some implications of Montaigne's warning to us.

Costs of Seeking Information

As with lunch, there is no such thing as free information. To get the information you need, you will have to pay something. Money is perhaps the most obvious cost of seeking information. Sometimes the monetary costs are direct and obvious. You need a reference book that is not in the library, so you go to the bookstore (or your computer) and buy it. If you want a consultant to do market research, you pay the person. If you want to find out why your customers are buying your product less and a competitor's product more, then you will do interviews or surveys or conduct focus groups. All of these options cost money, and the better, more sophisticated, and in-depth information seeking you do, the more it will cost. Sometimes the payment for information takes the form of a bribe. In what has become a movie cliché, a detective goes up to the hotel clerk and says he needs information about X person. The clerk looks blank, says it's hard to remember. The detective sighs, takes out his wallet, and says, "Let me help you clear up your memory." "Ah, now I remember," responds the clerk. "I thought you would," replies the detective.

But there are other costs of information seeking, costs that are sometimes overlooked, and it is to these costs that we now turn.

Information seeking and consequent information receiving constitute a potentially costly exchange relationship.

Social exchange is a critical factor in the stabilization of societies. As Marcel Mauss argued, exchange is governed by three obligations in social life: the obligation to give, to receive, and to repay.[38] How some of these exchange relationships work in our own society is discussed by Peter Blau in *Exchange and Power in Social Life*:

> If a person goes to some trouble in behalf of an acquaintance, he expects *some* expression of gratitude, but he can neither bargain with the other over how to reciprocate nor force him to reciprocate at all.
>
> Since there is no way to assure an appropriate return for a favor, social exchange requires trusting others to discharge their obligations. . . . Typically, however, exchange relations evolve in a slow process, starting with

minor transactions in which little trust is required because little risk is involved. A worker may help a colleague a few times. If the colleague fails to reciprocate, the worker has lost little and can easily protect himself against further loss by ceasing to furnish assistance. If the colleague does reciprocate, perhaps excessively out of gratitude for the volunteered help and in hope of receiving more, he proves himself trustworthy of continued and extended favors. (Excessive reciprocation may be embarrassing, because it is a bid for a more extensive exchange relation than one may be willing to enter.) By discharging their obligations for services rendered, if only to provide inducements for the supply of more assistance, individuals demonstrate their trustworthiness, and the gradual expansion of mutual service is accompanied by a parallel growth of mutual trust.[39]

We can think about exchange in terms of goods and commodities. A potlatch, as Mauss notes, is a means of distributing material wealth in the form of gifts. And we can think about exchange in terms of social interactions. For example, you invite a couple to your house for dinner. Some weeks later, the invitation is returned, and you go to their house for dinner. Information too is a commodity. It can be offered to you, just like any material gift, and it can be exchanged, just like any commodity or social interaction. The rules that govern social exchange apply with equal force to exchange relationships created by information exchange. If in exchange relationships there is an obligation to receive, and you deny that obligation (as well you might), you have to be prepared to accept the consequences. If you have to turn down an invitation to dinner, you will do so with some care and some sense of the consequences. You will offend the person who offers you dinner if you say abruptly, "I can't come to dinner at your house." The difficulties of saying "thanks, but no thanks" are commonly known. In similar manner, when people come to you with the gift of information, you have to make a critical decision as to whether to accept the gift or refuse it.

On one level, information exchange is simple reciprocity: I tell you something; you tell me something. Lord Chesterfield reminds us, "A man who tells nothing, or tells all, will equally have nothing told him."[40] I ask you for information about the inside politics of a university department. If I cannot give you something back on the spot, I will probably find a way to tell you that I am willing to return the favor in the future. If there is no reciprocation, then there is no exchange relationship, and before very long, I will find that you are unwilling to tell me anything.

A leader might well be willing to refuse to engage in the exchange relationship because he does not want the information that badly, or can get the information by other means, or does not want to tamper with the mystique of his presence, his imperturbability. Tacitus tells us of Tiberius, "Now that he was determined to show no sign of his real feelings, his words became more and more equivocal and obscure."[41] Elizabeth I's motto was *video et taceo* ("I see and am silent"). In Stendhal's *Lucien Leuwen*, we read the father's advice to the son: "One sees too much soul through your words. There's no lack of sense, but you talk too much of your feelings—far too much. It attracts every kind of rogue. So try and amuse people by talking about what doesn't interest you in the least."[42]

An interesting aspect of the reciprocity is that the parties involved have to have an agreement, if only a tacit one, of what is to constitute fair exchange. I ask you for information, and I have to give you some information back, but it cannot be just any information: it has to be information that you feel is of value. The exchange must be roughly equal from the point of view of both parties. A birthday party at the office will be going along fine, with most people giving gifts worth, say, twenty dollars. But then one person gives an emerald pendant worth many thousands of dollars. There will be embarrassment; the receiver will most likely be unwilling to accept the gift. The exchange will be out of balance, and everyone will know it. We calibrate these things very finely, and most of us have a good working sense of the kinds and values of gifts that are appropriate to various situations.

In order to keep the exchange relationship going, I have to seek further information to know whether what I am give you is going to "qualify" as repayment. If I am unwilling to repay in kind (or what is seen as a legitimate repayment), I have to decide whether I so badly want the information you have that I am willing to forgo a future exchange relationship, that is, whether I want short-term or long-term gains.

Another way of looking at this matter of information-seeking and exchange relationships is to view it in terms of capital. There is economic and financial capital, as we know. There is human capital. In recent years, there has been considerable attention devoted to social capital. And we can speak of information-seeking exchange capital: What are you willing to risk? What are you willing to expend? What kinds of relationships are you willing to establish or forgo?

Exchange relationships can be created quite unintentionally. If you let people know the time and date of a reception for a new staff member, you are also perhaps creating an expectation along with the information. Those who are receiving the information are not only receiving the information; they are receiving an implied expectation, unless you specifically say something to the effect that "I know you are busy and might not be able to attend."

Often the potential exchange relationship is unsolicited. Some years ago, I was looking for a new car, and all of my coworkers gave me advice. One person insisted I get a Buick, just like his—the best car in the world, he said. I ended up with a Toyota. By rejecting his advice, I was in some small way rejecting *him*. And here we are again reminded of the shrewdness of Machiavelli's advice in controlling who can give you information. Someone who gives you information unsolicited is in effect offering you a gift. That person is giving you the offer of a relationship—a relationship that you might not want but will nonetheless need to deal with.

We can see then that exchange relationships are quite complex. There is a delicate balance of giving, receiving, repaying. Montaigne has this to say on the matter of the delicate balance:

> When some years ago I read Philippe de Commines, certainly a very good author, I noted this remark as uncommon: "That we must be very careful not to serve our master so well that we keep him from finding a fair reward for our service." I should have praised the idea, not him; I came across it in Tacitus not long ago: "Benefits are agreeable as long as they seem returnable, but if they go much beyond that, they are repaid with hatred instead of gratitude." And Seneca says vigorously, "For he who thinks it is shameful not to repay does not want the man to live whom he ought to repay." Q. Cicero, in a weaker vein: "He who thinks he cannot repay you can by no means be your friend."[43]

From the perspective of the person who gives information to the leader, the admonitions of de Commines, Tacitus, Seneca, and Cicero have direct application. If in response to a leader's request for information, you give your leader so much of so great a value that the leader cannot possibly repay you, you might end up not with the leader's gratitude but with the leader's resentment. If information is a gift (even if requested), then one needs to be very careful to ensure that the gift does not become burdensome. Even on a lesser scale, one needs to be careful about excessiveness. If you prepare a sixty-page report in response to a simple request for a short list of suggested books, you might be seen as implying much more than hard work on your part. The recipient might wonder what you are up to. Are you trying to suggest in some sort of subtle way that the request was improperly limited? Are you trying to display your vast erudition? Are you displaying an odd kind of enthusiasm?

Information seeking is costly because it is path dependent.

Information seeking is path dependent: once it is under way, it can lead to other kinds of information seeking and an inability to stop. Moreover, information seeking is path dependent in that once having sought information by a given means from a given source, one is often precluded from seeking the same (confirming) information or additional information by other means from other sources.

The example from ancient times is again Oedipus. He starts the seeking of information as a perfectly rational course of action, trying to find out how to stop the plague, and once he starts, he is locked in. Tieresias is followed by Jocasta, who gives him information and tries to turn him away from looking further, in turn followed by the messenger, and then, finally, the herdsman and ultimate disaster.

George Orwell gives an example of path dependence in his essay "Shooting an Elephant." As a policeman in colonial Burma, Orwell is told about an elephant that has gone on a rampage, killing a local person. He goes to the scene, sees the dead man, and sees that the elephant is now quiet. He is armed with a small-caliber rifle, no match for the elephant. On the one hand, he feels obligated to do something about the elephant; on the other hand, the elephant no longer poses a threat. But Orwell lessens his options by taking a step, a path-dependent step: he sends for his larger-caliber rifle, one that is capable of bringing the elephant down. Once he has the gun, he feels he has little choice: he shoots the elephant (incompetently, and the elephant takes a long and painful time to die). Had Orwell not sent for the gun (a form of information, if you will), he would not have been locked into what he then saw as his only choice.

In *Shakespeare's Game*, William Gibson talks of path dependence in *Hamlet*:

It is as in chess, also an energy system, one move pro-
vokes another. Horatio, once he has seen the ghost,
must act; the move is his. It requires a decision, and he
can decide his eyes are failing and go off to the oculist,
or the Denmark fog is too much and go south for the
winter, but these decisions will take him and us into a
different game, not too inviting. In truth, he has no
choice, the one decision that moves this game forward
is "Let us impart what we have seen tonight unto young
Hamlet."[44]

Path dependence is a critical aspect of information seeking. Not
all of our situations will be as dramatic as Orwell's or Hamlet's, but
we can nonetheless inadvertently get ourselves locked in. Consider
a simple example. You seek information from Person A, who
promises to "get back to you soon." Let us say that after a reasonable period of time, you do not hear from Person A. You have several choices to make at this point. The first is to determine what
really is an acceptable "reasonable period of time." If you have a
deadline, that period of time might well be determined for you. The
second choice is whether to go back to Person A or to go to another
person for the information. If you go back to Person A with a
reminder that you really do need the information and you need it
very soon, Person A might see you as nagging or distrusting. If you
go to Person B seeking the same information, your problems are not
necessarily over. Person B might not give you the information any
faster than Person A might have. But let us say that Person B gives
you that information. Your problems still are not necessarily over.
Let us say that at long last, Person A comes back to you with the
information—information that Person A went to some considerable trouble to obtain. What do you say to Person A? Do you say
"thank you," not letting on that you already have the information?
If you do so, you might well get caught in a lie: Person A might

have already found out from Person B that you went elsewhere. (It might well be that Person B went to Person A, thinking that Person A was the logical source.) On other hand, if you let Person A know that you have sought and received the information from someone else, you might be seen as implying that Person A just could not be trusted to deliver the goods. Moreover, if Person A asks you where you got the information, then you have to either refuse to divulge your source (for whatever reason), which might cause bad feelings, or you let on that you sought the information from Person B, thus possibly making Person A feel resentful toward Person B.

All you did in the beginning, in this apparently simple example, was decide to seek information from Person A. Once you made the move to seek the information, you enmeshed yourself in a path-dependent situation, with some choices now open to you and other choices limited or no longer open.

Information seeking is costly because seeking information in itself provides information.

A principal in a school wants to develop a new program. She cannot do it by herself, she is not too sure whether it is the best choice, and ultimately she is going to need the support of most of the teachers in order to get the program off the ground. If she asks all of the staff what they think, she will be providing the information that she is thinking about the new program. But she does not want the entire staff in a buzz about something that might not even happen. So she decides to talk informally with two teachers about what she has in mind in order to get their opinions and needed information. This might seem to be a simple and straightforward gathering of information and testing the waters. But when she seeks the information from the two teachers rather than the entire group, she is nevertheless providing the information that she is thinking about a new program. The principal, being prudent, will have to conduct some sort of probability assessment. If she wants to keep the program she has in mind as a possibility and not something to be seen as a fait accompli, she has to assume that the two teachers she talks with will be able to keep quiet and not gossip. Again, as with Lord Chesterfield, there are people who will tell secrets because they have a vanity in showing that "they have been, though very undeservedly, trusted."

As another example, a student is thinking about taking a given course in graduate school and decides to seek information from the professor who will be teaching the course. By seeking information about course content, the student is providing the information that she is thinking about enrolling. There is a possible advantage here in that if the student actually enrolls, she might be seen by the professor as a rational, thoughtful person, an impression that the student might find useful. On the other hand, if the student decides not to enroll, there is the possibility—even ever so slight—of hurt feelings, and if the graduate department in question is small, with no place to hide, there might be some tension. Thus, the student might decide that rather than seeking information from the professor, she will rely on other students to give her useful information about the course.

It is often important to seek information specifically to provide information. Early on in World War II, the British, with the help of Polish mathematicians, cracked the German high command cipher codes through the capture of the Germans' Enigma coding machines. It is a great advantage to know where your enemy is planning to attack. But the British and, later, the other Allies could not forthrightly act on the information they now had. If the Allies massed troops and planes in anticipation of an attack, the Germans would have realized that the only way the Allies could have anticipated the attack was that they had cracked the command codes. Accordingly, the Allies had to maintain other obvious sources of information seeking. The location of a German battleship, although known in advance through Engima messages, had to be seen by the Germans as being determined by British search planes. Moreover, throughout the war, the Allies continued to act as if they were seeking information about how to crack the code in order to avoid providing the information that they had already done so.[45] From time to time, German military officers suspected that their codes had been broken, but they had enough confidence in the security of the system that they rejected the possibility of successful decipherment.

A similar, and costly, pride was shown by both the German and Japanese military command. Early in the war, a highly placed German spy informed Berlin and Tokyo that the Americans had cracked the Japanese military codes, but the information was rejected out of misplaced pride: they could not believe that their "sophisticated and well-guarded Signals Intelligence code in fact could ever be broken."[46]

A new leader's information-seeking priorities exemplifies a critical aspect of information seeking and providing. A school's new principal has just come on board. People are wondering, as is always the case with a new leader, what is going to happen, what is going to change. Everyone is watching, seeking information themselves on what kinds of information the principal first seeks (and, just as important, what the principal appears to be ignoring). If, within the first week, the principal is asking for comprehensive data on enrollment of girls in advanced math and science classes and summaries of Title IX reports, the staff will have fairly good reason to believe that Title IX is going to be taken seriously. The alert and prudent principal will take advantage of this aspect of information seeking and provision. She might outline her priorities in an inaugural address to the staff, but she will reinforce the message of the importance of those priorities by being clearly manifest in what she chooses to seek information about.

When you seek information, there is often the danger that you will end up providing a lot more information than you wanted to. For example, if you call up central administration to find out when a report is due, you are giving someone in the central office the information that you have not completed your report.

Sometimes your seeking of information will provide the information that you are anxious about the result. You might well be anxious, but you do not necessarily want to let the anxiety show. You forward a funding proposal to a foundation and wait to hear whether it has been approved. Months pass. You want to know what's what. If the foundation is going to turn it down, you can go elsewhere, but you have to be very careful in seeking information about the status of your proposal. You do not want to appear anxious, and thus have your anxiety communicate insecurity. Nor do you want to appear pushy or censorious. The mere seeking of a response to "What's happening to our proposal?" can be seen as implying that you think the foundation is perhaps a bit slow off the mark, or implying that the staff *should* be working on something they are not.

Sometimes you can provide information by not appearing to seek enough information. A physician examines a patient. The physician can tell a great deal about the patient's condition by simple observation. But the patient might feel that the physician does not really care, is not paying close attention, and will get angry—sometimes angry enough to write letters of complaint to hospital administrators about cold, unfeeling physicians who do not care about patients. When confronted with such patients, some physicians will make an elaborate show of seeking information and conduct additional and unnecessary tests simply to help patients feel that they are being treated properly.

Seeking information about a problem can heighten awareness of a problem, and the implications of seeking and providing can be profound. If you send out a survey to employees to assess perceptions of your company's child care facilities, you will be providing the information that you are for one reason or another at least thinking about the possible need to do something about the facilities. Your seeking the information very possibly will raise expectations. Had you not sought the information, the employees might not have realized that the facilities were a possible agenda item. As Tocqueville tells us, once you start to ameliorate conditions (and information seeking will often be seen as the beginning of amelioration), you will be in a tenuous position:

> The most perilous moment for a bad government is one when it seeks to mend its ways. Only consummate statecraft can enable a King to save his throne when after a long spell of oppressive rule he sets to improving the lot of his subjects. Patiently endured so long as it seemed beyond redress, a grievance comes to appear intolerable once the possibility of removing it crosses men's minds. For the mere fact that certain abuses have been remedied draws attention to the others, and they now appear more galling; people may suffer less, but their sensibility is exacerbated.[47]

It should be noted that you can raise expectations not only for others but for yourself. For example, I found that when I ordered a computer on-line, the company's sophisticated tracking system provided me information on a real-time basis, allowing me to follow the stages of ordering, processing, and shipping. But perhaps there was too much provision of information. When the computer was not delivered the minute they said it would be, I became a bit irritated, feeling the company had not kept up its part of the bargain. Had we been back in the old, pre-Internet days, I would not have known with such precision what was supposed to be going on. As long as the computer was delivered in a three-day range of what the company had promised, I would have been happy.

Information seeking entails potentially costly ethical questions.

Sometimes you do not want to seek information. Richard Breitman's exhaustive analysis of British war records finally declassified in 1997 indicates that the British and American intelligence and military command knew at the time a great deal of the Nazi plans for the elimination of the Jews of Europe. They knew but chose not to acknowledge their knowledge. As a review noted, Breitman's book reveals a "startling nonchalance in facing evil."[48] Sometimes maybe you will want to deny information that someone wishes to provide you (or you will not seek the information actively) because if you know, you will be in ethical difficulties. "Don't ask, don't tell," is not a policy or strategy that applies solely to gay people in the military.

Again, we can advert to George Orwell's situation described in "Shooting an Elephant." Sending for the elephant gun is a critical move that Orwell made, one that gets him into trouble. Sending for the gun is in effect like seeking information, and sometimes you would be far better off not to seek the information in the first place.

Sometimes when you seek information, people will expect you to do something with the information you are trying to gather. If, for example, you seek information from a group of workers about their perceptions of working conditions, you had best be prepared to tell them what you plan to do with the responses. In this situation, you have an ethical obligation to provide information even as you seek information.

If you have the information and you are seen to have it, then you might have to do something with it. For example, if a school district disaggregates its test scores by the variables of ethnicity and socioeconomic status and the results show significant differences in test scores on the basis of those variables and the results are published, then there might well be pressure on the district. Once you know and are seen to know the inequities, a reasonable question people might ask is what you are going to do about the situation.

Sometimes it is better not to seek information, at least not publicly, because you do not know what you might have to do with the information you get. All lawyers know never to ask a question without knowing what the response is going to be.

Conclusion

Leaders who wish to persuade must seek information on which to base their presumably persuasive appeals. Moreover, they must seek information while making those appeals and afterward, to gauge the effectiveness of the work. Given the discussion of information-seeking principles, strategies, and costs, it is clear that leaders have before them here an extraordinarily difficult endeavor. Part of this endeavor can be better prosecuted if leaders consider and act on the following seven cautions:

1. Do not shoot the messenger.
2. Reward people who give you good information.
3. Be prepared to give as well as receive information.
4. Do not allow your optimism to shut out negative information.
5. Do not allow your negativity to disallow positive information.
6. Do not accept or reject information solely on the basis of the source.
7. Be wary of exchange relationships and traps.

These cautions notwithstanding, leaders need to realize that information seeking is fraught with political and ethical dilemmas. The seven cautions will not suffice: leaders must weigh and consider the conditions under which they might want to dissemble in order to obtain or withhold information and the conditions under which they might or might not want to enter into possibly fraudulent relationships with others in order to obtain the information they think they want. As we will note in Chapter Three, there is an ecology of ideas, and there surely is an ecology of relationships that can be supported or harmed by the means by which we seek information.

3

The Ethics and Ecology
of Persuasion

Information seeking inevitably raises questions of ethics. You can,
should you so desire, seek information by spying, or stealing, or
torturing, or blackmailing informants. Most of us will say that such
means are unethical. We can try to keep our information seeking
ethical—straightforward, no lies, no subterfuge, above board, not
hurtful to ourselves or to others—assuming we can do so. We still
have many ethical questions to deal with when we turn from information seeking to the next step: the persuasion of others. There are,
moreover, ecological questions to deal with as well, given that how
we choose to persuade others is connected to the larger political
environment.

The Ethics of Persuasion

It might seem obvious that seeking information can be an ethical
matter. But what of persuasion more largely? To address this question, we have to consider the relationship between choices and
ethics, and we have to think of persuasion of a form of action with
choices. Not all actions are of ethical import. In Book Three of the
Ethics, Aristotle makes careful distinctions between involuntary and
voluntary actions, and further distinctions between voluntary
actions stemming from desire or temper, and actions stemming from

choice. "What is chosen is voluntary, but not everything that is voluntary is chosen. Well, is it the result of previous deliberation? For choice implies a rational principle, and thought. The name, too, seems to indicate something that is chosen *before* other things." Aristotle argues that "what we deliberate about is practical measures that lie within our power" and that "since, therefore, an object of choice is something within our power at which we aim after deliberation, choice will be a deliberate appetition of things that lie in our power."[1] Machiavelli makes a similar distinction with his observation that "men act from necessity or from choice."[2] And Immanuel Kant reminds us that "a free will and a will subject to moral laws are one and the same."[3] William James suggests that "ascending still higher, we reach the plane of Ethics, where choice reigns notoriously supreme. An act has no ethical quality whatever unless it be chosen out of several all equally possible. . . . The ethical energy *par excellence* has to go further and choose which *interest* out of several, equally coercive, shall become supreme. . . . The problem with the man is less what act he shall now choose to do, than what being he shall now resolve to become."[4] In a slightly different vein, Montaigne quotes Cicero, "Even a just action is just only so far as it is voluntary," and Montaigne goes on to say that "if the action does not have something of the splendor of freedom, it has neither grace nor honor."[5]

For a matter to be of ethical import, it must be a matter of choice. We do not look at someone and say, "Look how tall she is. Isn't she *ethical* because she's so tall?" She did not choose to get tall. She had no choice in the matter. So her tallness is not of ethical import. We can say, though, "Look how kind she is to other people. Isn't she ethical because she's so kind?" Or, "Look how nasty she is to others. Isn't she unethical, given her nastiness?" To put it another way, if we remove the capability of a person to commit a crime, then the *non*-crime behavior of that person cannot be considered ethical per se because there was no choice.

There has to be choice if the matter is to have ethical import. But not all choices necessarily have ethical implications. Choosing between red and black jelly beans does not bear on matters ethical. As John Dewey put it, "Choice would hardly be significant if it did not take effect in outward action, and if it did not when expressed in deeds make a difference in things."[6] Choices are ethical matters when they involve deliberation of practicable means to an end.

We have at the very least three choices to make when we engage in persuasion. First, we have to make choices regarding the ordering of the goods. What is it that we think should be? Second, we have to make choices about the kind or form of arguments to be used. Should we argue on the basis of principle, or interest, or greed, or revenge, or honor? Third, we have to make choices about how we are going to talk. Should we speak passionately or coldly, softly or with raised voice, slowly or rapidly, with simple words and sentences or with complexity?

Let us consider these three choices that we have to make when we undertake to persuade others and examine how the choices have ethical considerations.

Persuasion and Ordering of the Goods

Persuasion is a form of rhetoric. Some, as with Aristotle, would argue that rhetoric is above all concerned with persuasion: "Rhetoric may be defined as the faculty of observing in any given case the available means of persuasion,"[7] and, as Francis Bacon argues, that "the duty and office of rhetoric is, to apply reason to imagination to the better moving of the will."[8] Better moving suggests more than effectiveness. Richard Weaver argues that "rhetoric seen in the whole conspection of its function is an art of emphasis embodying an order of desire. Rhetoric is advisory; it has the office of advising men with reference to an independent order of goods and with reference to their particular situation as it relates to these. The honest rhetorician therefore has two things in mind: a vision of how matters should go ideally and ethically and a consideration of the special circumstances of his auditors."[9] Furthermore, Weaver tells us, "a rhetoric without some vision of the order of the goods is actually a contradiction in terms; it would have nowhere to go, nothing to do. We cannot be too energetic in reminding our nihilists and positivists that this is a world of action and history, and that all policies involve choosing between better and worse."[10] And, finally, Weaver reminds us that "just as no action is really indifferent, so no utterance is without its responsibility."[11]

As Walter Beale suggests, "Rhetorical education is an attempt to shape a certain kind of character capable of using language effectively to carry on the practical and moral business of a polity. It is based implicitly on ideals of individual competence and political well-being. Its dual purposes are the cultivation of the individual and the success of a culture."[12]

The process of persuasion is in effect a worldview—an ordering of the goods, a choice between better and worse, and, beyond that, an understanding of how we do the ordering and how we talk about it. Thus, a basic question for all rhetoricians is one of epistemology. As P. Albert Duhamel puts it, "The rhetorician's conception of the value of argument, the process of invention by which arguments are to be discovered, the extent to which the devices of elocution are to be employed, is the result of his evaluation of the reliability of the intellect, the nature and availability of truth, and the existence of certitude. . . . Thus Aristotle was preoccupied with the erection of a system of rhetoric which would discover and express probabilities; Plato valued only the Absolute."[13]

When we attempt to persuade, then, we are making—and offering to others—a choice of a worldview.

Following are some examples of ordering of the goods, of asking people to choose between the better and the worse. A politician tells us that schools are in bad shape, and we need to get students' scores up on the statewide tests. Here is a clear ordering of goods, a vision of the world, and an epistemology all neatly packaged together. To say that schools are bad is to say, directly or indirectly, what good schools are (something to do with test scores, apparently), and that in the world we would prefer, there would be schools and schools would be attending to the teaching of something that can be measured by means of paper-and-pencil tests, and we would "know" whether schools were achieving the good we desire by comparing test scores.

As another plain example, the school board decides to allocate additional monies to the athletic program, and thus not additional monies to the debate program. Budget is policy, and policy is a choice among alternatives. Whether the board wishes to argue that the choice is between two equally worthy goods, or between the lesser of two evils, or better or worse, the board is still making a choice of practicable means to an end. When asked by parents and other community members about the budget, board members will have to have recourse to an ordering of the goods.

Persuasion and Selection of Arguments

It is difficult enough to settle on a given policy or a given course of action to follow, but there are still other difficult choices to make. There are many ways in which to convince others to follow that policy or course of action. There are many ways to talk, many ways to argue. You have to make choices. We have already noted choices of action that are not acceptable. Again, force is not persuasion. But there are many ways to engage in speech that attempts to persuade by nonforceful means. And whatever way we choose to talk will have profound implications.

For example, if your child asks, "Why should I love Grandma?" you could reply, "Because she has a lot of money, and if you're nice to her, she'll leave it to you in her will." Or you could reply, "Because she's your grandma." Both responses ask for the same behavior—loving Grandma—but the one response constitutes a calculative relationship and thus, ultimately, a calculative society, and the other constitutes a normative relationship and a normative society.

Or, for example, consider the responses you might make to a student asking you why she should study. A considerable array of arguments can be invoked. Why should you study? Because I'll hit you if you don't. Because you will become a better person. Because you will make me sad (or angry, or ashamed) if you don't. Because I want you to be able to get a good job. Because you will become self-actualized. Because you'll find the subject matter of intrinsic interest. Each of these responses contains in itself an argument, a view of the world, a vision of the good. If the only way I think I can get you to study is to hit you, that is saying a great deal about me, you, and what I think about the world. It is not a pleasant world I am constituting and offering when I have to hit you to "persuade" you (and, as we noted in Chapter One, force is not persuasion in the first place). Left unspoken, with such an argument or threat, is whether what is supposed to be studied has any meaning or relevance here at all or whether obedience is sufficient. To argue in terms of instrumental payoff—study hard in order to get a good job—might seem persuasive (at least it is not brute force) as a rational choice resulting in money and other goods, but the silence as to the possible intrinsic rewards of studying suggests a willingness to consider the world solely in economic terms. Each of the other arguments for studying implies a particular way to constitute the world. (It might be noted that where we are talking about choice of argument here, others might use other terminology, such as *story* or *narrative*. The terminology might differ, but the notion holds. For example, to speak of an "economic narrative" of schooling is to be making a series of choices of ways of arguing, of constituting and explaining the world.)

So we can advocate a given behavior for a host of different reasons and with greatly different consequences. In *The Rebel*, Albert Camus notes that "to live is also to act. To act in the name of what?"[14] We need to ask ourselves what we act in the *name* of. We need to consider the different kinds of arguments, the different ways of speaking, when we speak in the name of something.

"We think about those things that offer us alternative possibil-ities," Aristotle says.[15] Perhaps. But sometimes we choose among alternatives without a good deal of thought. We choose a line of argument, a way of talking and reasoning and persuading, without, sometimes, a great deal of attention. And sometimes the choice we make is not even a conscious choice; we talk a certain way out of habit. What we need to do is reflect on how we talk. One way of re-flecting on how we talk is to consider some of the basic kinds of arguments we can make when trying to persuade others.

Choice of Arguments

Given that speech that is intended to persuade—to move to belief or action—is directed to a specific audience at a specific time, with specific circumstances and priorities already established, human beings are not to be separated from that context, nor are they likely to be persuaded solely by rational discourse or logic. It is thus that Aristotle (and a host of others following him) placed such empha-sis not only on logic but on emotions and feelings, and the audi-ence's estimate of the speaker. Beyond choice of balance between or combination of logos, pathos, and ethos, there are many kinds of arguments, many ways to choose to appeal to an audience.[16] We will consider four basic kinds of argument.

One kind is an argument from definition or genus. We speak of the nature of the thing—a nature that is presumed to persist and not be altered. In *The Federalist* No. 10, James Madison argues that "the latent causes of faction are thus sown in the nature of man; and we see them every where brought into different degrees of activity, according to the different circumstances of society." In *The Federalist* No. 51, he gives another example of argument from defi-nition: "Ambition must be made to counteract ambition. The inter-est of the man must be connected with the constitutional rights of the place. It may be a reflection on human nature, that such devices should be necessary to controul the abuses of government. But what is government itself but the greatest of all reflections on human nature? If men were angels, no government would be necessary."[17] In much of his writing, Abraham Lincoln used a fundamental argument from definition. As Richard Weaver suggests, Lincoln's "refusal to hedge on the principle of slavery is referable to a fixed concept of the nature of man."[18]

A second kind of argument is similitude (and dissimilitude). Something not known very well is said to be similar to something known much better, and if the one is like the other in some respects, it is probable that it is like the other in other respects. For example, teacher leaders have often used an argument from similitude in making claims to be professionals: we are like doctors in that we do thus and so; therefore, we should be accorded the same sort of respect and privilege accorded doctors generally.[19]

Third, we can argue from consequence. The argument depends on establishing a cause-and-effect relationship, as in, "If you elect me, your taxes will be cut," or, "If you elect my unworthy and venal opponent, we will have another Great Depression."

Fourth, we can argue from circumstance. The argument seeks not principle or similitude or even cause and effect, but rather relies on the brutal facts of the moment. In plain form, the argument is, "Given the situation, what else can we do?" An argument from circumstance focuses on what you are stuck with in the immediate here and now, as opposed to an argument from consequence that at least attempts a look into (or a hedge against) something in the future.

In discussing the forms of argument and their implications, Richard Weaver puts forth a suggestive argument of his own. Weaver claims that "a man's method of argument is a truer index in his beliefs than his explicit profession of principles. Here is a means whereby he is revealed in his work." The "choice of one's source of argument," Weaver says, is "the most critical undertaking of all" (strong words from such a careful writer!). Moreover, he notes, "Nowhere does a man's rhetoric catch up with him more completely than in the topics he chooses to win other men's assent."[20]

For Weaver, the kinds of arguments differ considerably in terms of philosophical and ethical weight. He argues that for the most part, an argument from definition or genus is superior philosophically to an argument from circumstance. Lincoln, Weaver suggests, tended to rely on arguments from definition, which tends to peg him as a true conservative (at least by Weaver's definition, as one concerned with human nature and basic principles), whereas Edmund Burke, later to be adopted as a hero of the conservatives, tended to argue from circumstance and thus had little solid grounding and should not be taken as an exemplar for conservatives. Applying Weaver's approach to our earlier example, we can see that telling a child to love her grandma in order to receive money is an argument from consequence, and not a very edifying one at that; telling a child to love her grandma "because she's your grandma" is looking for bedrock, an argument from definition.

Others have made distinctions similar to those noted by Weaver. Winston Churchill identified the significance of arguing from principle rather than circumstance: "Those who are possessed of a definite doctrine and of deeply rooted convictions upon it will be in a much better position to deal with the shifts and surprises of daily affairs than those who are merely taking short views, and indulging their natural impulses as they are evoked by what they read from day to day."[21] And Churchill would no doubt have approved of Tocqueville's observation, "What I call great political parties are those that are attached more to principles than to their consequences; to generalities and not to particular cases; to ideas and not to men."[22]

Thus, Richard Weaver suggests, "Other parties take their bearing from some philosophy of man and society; the Whigs take their bearing from the other parties. Whatever a party of left or right proposes, they propose (or oppose) in tempered measure. Its politics is then cautionary, instinctive, trusting more to safety and to present success than to imagination and dramatic boldness of principle. It is, to make the estimate candid, a politics without vision, and consequently without the capacity to survive."[23]

An example of how one's choice of argument can lead to perilous results can be seen in the sometimes popular way to argue for such programs as the visual and performing arts in the schools. Some say that the best way to argue for school arts programs is to claim that arts are an inherent part of the human condition, and as part of being human, we should be exposed to them. That argument will not persuade people, say the "realists," given the current emphasis on testing and accountability. We have to argue from consequence, they say: put an arts program in your high school, and test scores will go up. The argument from consequence here is a dangerous one, given that it is notoriously difficult to link test scores to other variables, and even if an evaluation study showed a significant correlation, naysayers could always argue that the evaluation methodology was inadequate or faulty. Moreover, there is a reasonable chance that test scores will go down.

Some years ago, I happened to hear a similarly structured argument from a school district official. The district had just embarked on a major school desegregation program. The official told a community group that we would know whether the desegregation plan was a good thing if test scores went up. This argument from consequence was exceedingly shaky, given the odds that test scores would likely remain the same or regress. A much more powerful argument came from a school board member in the same district, who had said in court that they had desegregated the schools because it was the right thing to do—an argument from definition.

Both the "arts will raise test scores" and "desegregation is good if test scores go up" are examples of Weaver's "politics without vision," without "the capacity to survive."

Weaver's argument is suggestive, even if we do not accept it as applying equally in all circumstances.[24] It may be that one form of argument is not necessarily superior ethically to another in all cir-cumstances. Argument from definition or basic principle will not always keep you on solid ground. *Les Misérables* offers a telling example. Jean Valjean is pursued by police inspector Javert. The inspector is governed by a basic principle: the law is the law and must be upheld at all costs—a reasonable notion about the law, this argument from definition. But Javert steadfastly ignores any con-sideration of circumstance, any consideration of justice tempered by mercy. In the end, his argument from definition is not an argu-ment but an idée fixe. Javert cannot deal with the contradiction between his argument from definition and his underlying feelings of humanness toward Jean Valjean (who, after all, spared Javert's life). He resolves the contradiction by committing suicide. (We might note too that officious bureaucrats often operate from a Javert-like argument from definition of regulations.)

A poignant instance of sticking to principle as an argument is found in Ingmar Bergman's 1957 film, *Wild Strawberries*. An old curmudgeon, Isak Borg, has loaned money to his son for medical school expenses. His daughter-in-law points out that she and her husband have had to work overly hard to pay back the money, money the old man does not need. Isak is unperturbed. "Although I realize it's difficult for him, a bargain is a bargain," he says, and he knows that his son "understands and respects" him. His daughter-in-law returns with, "That may be true, but he also hates you." The argument is so strong that even near the end of the film, with Isak trying to bring up the subject of the "bargain" (with an intent to forgive the debt), his son interrupts him, saying, "Don't worry, you'll get your money." Isak protests, "I didn't mean that," but Evald responds, "You'll get your money all right."[25] There are similar examples of arguments from definition getting in the way of understanding other, larger issues in Barbara Tuchman's *In Praise of Folly*, ranging from the Protestant Succession and the British loss of the colonies to the U.S. prosecution of the war in Vietnam.[26]

But overall, Weaver's distinctions are critical. What are the ethical implications of these different ways of arguing? Or, to paraphrase James Boyd White, what kind of a world do you claim and constitute when you choose a given form of argument? What kind of character do you define for yourself? What kind of character do you offer to others when you choose to talk one way rather than another?[27] Moreover, what kind of character are you attributing to your audience when you talk one way rather than another?

If you offer your audience a bribe of one sort or another, you are saying, "I know you. I know that you will not be moved by ethics or principles, but I do know you will be moved by the possibility of riches." If you suggest to your staff that blackmail will be useful in neutralizing an opponent, you are stating that you think blackmail is appropriate behavior and you think your staff does too. On the other hand, if you spend a great deal of time with your staff looking for an argument that will not only be "effective" but is also on ethical high ground, your staff will respond accordingly.

We do have to think about these things that offer alternative possibilities. Every choice of argument constitutes the world.

Choices of Facts and Issues

There are more choices to make in constructing arguments. You have to choose which facts and issues you want to bring to bear. (Again, note the verb *choose*, with all the implications again of ethical matters.) You cannot say everything about everything. You will have to be selective, focusing on some facts and issues (and perhaps on what you think will work), and you will necessarily have to ignore other facts and issues (including perhaps those that you think will damage your case).

One kind of choice to make stems from the need to sort out the consequential from the unimportant. As Edmund Burke suggests,

> To complain of the age we live in, to murmur at the present possessors of power, to lament the past, to conceive

extravagant hopes of the future, are the common dispositions of the greatest part of mankind; indeed the necessary effects of the ignorance and levity of the vulgar. Such complaints and humors have existed in all times; yet as all times have *not* been alike, true political sagacity manifests itself in distinguishing that complaint which only characterizes the general infirmity of human nature, from those which are symptoms of the particular distemperature of our own air and season.[28]

It is difficult to sort through the facts and issues, especially when we have so much information at our disposal. "Microscopes and telescopes really confuse a man's clear sense of sight," said Goethe.[29]

There are practical consequences and dangers associated with being too unselective. That wonderfully shrewd observer Samuel Johnson listens to an argument for being perhaps less selective than need be in trying to make a case:

> *Goldsmith.* "If you put a tub full of blood into a stable, the horses are like to go mad." *Johnson.* "I doubt that." *Goldsmith.* "Nay, Sir, it is a fact well authenticated." *Thrale.* "You had better prove it before you put it in your book on natural history. You may do it in my stable if you will." *Johnson.* "Nay, Sir, I would not have him prove it. If he is content to take his information from others, he may get through his book with little trouble, and without endangering his reputation. But if he makes experiments for so comprehensive a book as his, there would be no end of them; his erroneous assertions would then fall upon himself; and he might be blamed for not having made experiments as to every particular."[30]

Johnson's observation is on the mark. If we choose to select and support claims at a given level of specificity in some areas but not others, we lay ourselves open to the reader or auditor to ask why we are proving the perhaps inconsequential in some areas while leaving perhaps more important areas unattended.

Another kind of choice that must be made is when to avoid saying something out of prudence or fearing to offend colleagues or ruling powers. "The enjoyment of power is fatal to the subtleties of life," observed Alfred North Whitehead.[31] Indeed. In the original (1781) version *The Robber,* Schiller has Karl kill Amelia rather than forsake his gang. In 1782, at the request of a wealthy patron, Schiller changed the story: in the end, instead of killing Amelia, he marries her!

Chris Patten, former governor of Hong Kong, found that his publisher dropped plans to publish his memoir because of complaints from the company's owner, Rupert Murdoch, that Patten took a negative view of China. This was not the first time that Murdoch involved himself in such matters. "In a similar move in 1994 to avoid irritating the Chinese Government, he removed the BBC news service from his Hong Kong-based satellite service, Star TV, after Bejing protested its coverage of Chinese dissidents."[32]

What to put on the table, what to talk about, is a matter of power. In "One out of Twelve: Writers Who Are Women in Our Century," Tillie Olsen notes that "women's books of great worth suffer the death of being unknown, or at best a peculiar eclipsing, far outnumbering the similar fate of the few such books by men."[33]

Persuasion and Choosing How to Talk

The third choice to make focuses on style—on how we are going to talk. Of the many aspects of style, we can best look at four: terminology; euphemism and clear language; sentence structure, order, and syntax; and tone and delivery.

Terminology

How we choose to name things is of critical importance. Richard Weaver notes that "teaching people to speak the truth . . . can only be done by giving them the right names of things." Weaver reminds us that early on, Adam is involved in the naming of things: "And out of the ground the Lord God formed every beast of the field, and every fowl of the air, and brought them unto Adam to see what he would call them; and whatever Adam called every living creature, that was the name thereof." The names stuck: "A name is not just an accident; neither is it a convention which can be repealed by majority vote at the next meeting; once a thing has been given a name, it appears to have a certain autonomous right to that name, so that it could not be changed without imperiling the foundations of the world."[34] The world has to be named, and as Plato tells us, names have to be taught by teachers.[35] More recently, Lewis Carroll's Humpty Dumpty has this to say:

> "When I use a word," Humpty Dumpty said, in a rather scornful tone, "it means just what I choose it to mean— neither more nor less."
>
> "The question is," said Alice, "whether you *can* make words mean so many different things."
>
> "The question is," said Humpty Dumpty, "which is to be master—that's all."[36]

In *Standing by Words*, Wendell Berry reflects on the "gradual increase in language that is either meaningless or destructive of meaning." He reminds us that

> in order for a statement to be complete and comprehensible three conditions are required:
> 1. It must designate its object precisely.
> 2. Its speaker must be willing to stand by it: must believe it, be accountable for it, be willing to act on it.
> 3. This relation of speaker, word, and object must be conventional: the community must know what it is.[37]

Berry talks too of "precision of definition, this setting of bounds or ends to thought [without which] we cannot mean, or say what we mean, or mean what we say; we cannot stand by our words because we cannot utter words that can be stood by."[38]

Berry's concern about precision is shared by Tocqueville. In reflecting on how "democracy has modified the English language," Tocqueville notes that innovation in language "consists in giving to an expression already in use a sense not in use." Meaning is piled on meaning, with "no common arbitrator, no permanent tribunal, that can fix the sense of the word definitively," and thus word meaning is "left in a mobile situation." As for himself, Tocqueville says, "I would rather that the language be bristling with Chinese, Tartar, or Huron words than that the sense of French words be rendered uncertain. . . . There is no good language without clear terms." Tocqueville notes too the predilection of those in a democracy for abstract terms. Given mobility and the changing situation in a democracy, people must "have very large expressions" to contain their thoughts: "As they never know if the idea they are expressing today will suit the new situation they will have tomorrow, they naturally conceive a taste for abstract terms. An abstract word is like a box with a false bottom: one puts in it the ideas one desires and one takes them out without anyone's seeing it."[39]

In our own time, we can observe careful attention to terminology, as suggested by the following four examples.

Perhaps no one else understood better the subtleties of language and terminology than Winston Churchill. In addition to the marvelous stirring speeches of 1940—speeches that held Britain together at a time when many were ready to give up—Churchill paid close attention to small details, as evidenced in his concern over the "Home Guard" terminology, shortly after taking office in 1940. The volunteers working throughout the country at various tasks had been given the somewhat uninspiring title of "Local Defence Volunteers." Churchill proposed "Home Guard." Despite

Anthony Eden's opposition that "LDV" had already passed into current usage and had been "woven into a million brassards," Churchill held his ground (and would one have expected less of him?), and the "more simple and better name of 'Home Guard'" was born.[40]

The second example emerges from the Seattle school district's lengthy battle over school desegregation during the late 1970s. The proposed plan was termed "mandatory busing" by opponents, while supporters said the plan featured a "fixed assignment" strategy. The opponents fastened on the adjective "mandatory" with some success, given all the negative freight of that term in a nation that prides itself on freedom and rugged individualism. The supporters selected "fixed assignment" perhaps because the phrase sounds benign and conjures up no negative images (rather, one might argue, "fixed" implies a certain virtuous solidity), when in fact a student assigned to a certain school most assuredly would be paired with another school in another part of town and would indeed be transported, like it or not, to that school.

The third example of the power of terminology comes to us from the world of physics and physicist Stephen Hawking, who "came to prominence just at a time when John Wheeler, an American physicist, had coined the science-fiction-friendly term, black hole. 'It was,' Wheeler wrote later, a 'terminologically trivial but psychologically powerful' description. Hawking, author of the equally-powerful titled 'A Brief History of Time,' . . . noted: 'The importance in science of a good name should not be underestimated.'"[41]

The fourth example of the importance of names, modest but telling, comes from a small college in western Pennsylvania. The institution recently changed its name from Beaver College to Arcadia University, "aiming to shed a source of ridicule and boost enrollment." The new name was chosen based on surveys of thousands of alumni and parents, with a short list sent to focus groups.[42]

We might well conclude that the importance of names, good names, should not be underestimated in any human endeavor.

Euphemisms and Distancing Language

Euphemisms and distancing language are reflections of disconnection between words and meaning. In a justly famous description of the revolution at Corcyra, Thucydides gives us a sense of what happens when the connection between words and meaning becomes loosened:

> Words had to change their meaning and to take that which was now given them. Reckless audacity came to be considered the courage of a loyal ally; prudent hesitation, specious cowardice; moderation was held to be a cloak for unmanliness; ability to see all sides of a question inaptness to act on any. Frantic violence became the attribute of manliness; cautious plotting, a justifiable means of self-defence. The advocate of extreme measures was always trustworthy; his opponent a man to be suspected. To succeed in a plot was to have a shrewd head, to divine a plot still shrewder; but to try to provide against having to do either was to break up your party and to be afraid of your adversaries.[43]

George Orwell spends considerable time in *1984* and in *Animal Farm* dealing with euphemisms and the disconnect between words and meaning. Perhaps, though, his strongest statement comes from his oft-reprinted essay, "Politics and the English Language":

> In our time, political speech and writing are largely the defence of the indefensible. . . . Political language has to consist largely of euphemism, question-begging and sheer cloudy vagueness. Defenceless villages are bombarded from the air, the inhabitants driven out into the countryside, the cattle machine-gunned, the huts set on fire with incendiary bullets: this is called *pacification*. . . .

The great enemy of clear language is insincerity. When there is a gap between one's real and one's declared aims, one turns as it were instinctively to long words and exhausted idioms, like a cuttlefish squirting out ink. In our age there is no such thing as "keeping out of politics." All issues are political issues, and politics itself is a mass of lies, evasions, folly, hatred and schizophrenia. When the general atmosphere is bad, language must suffer. . . . But if thought corrupts language, language can also corrupt thought. A bad usage can spread by tradition and imitation, even among people who should and do know better.[44]

What can happen to language when euphemism comes into place is nicely illustrated by Lope de Vega in his play *Fuenteovejuna*, with one character telling us that "the blind man is said to be myopic, or, if you squint, you have a slight cast in one eye. A man with a wooden leg is a trifle lame, and a careless spendthrift a good chap. An ignorant ass is said to be the silent type, a braggart is known as soldierly." Well, another character replies, that may be so in the city, but here "a grave man is a bore. . . . If you are just, you are called cruel, if merciful, then you are weak. One who is constant is called boorish, the polite man is a flatterer, one who gives alms, a hypocrite."[45]

In *Dog Years*, Günter Grass comments at length on how the Nazis used obscurantist language to avoid facing complicity in evil. Grass imagines the German army chasing a dog: "The Nothing will be after-accomplished on the double. Each and every activity of the Nothing attuned to distantiality will be substantivized in view of final victory so that later, sculptured in marble or in shell-lime, it may be at-hand in a state of to-be-viewedness."[46] The Bolsheviks famously indulged in their own alterations of language: "Jocose euphemisms were coined for the business of killing: 'to send to a meeting,' 'to dispatch to Dukhonin's headquarters' (with reference to General N. N. Dukhonin, lynched by soldiers in late 1917), 'to put into an envelope and mail,' the last signifying to arrest and then execute."[47]

Albert Camus, no stranger to language, lies, and oppression, argued that "since the man who lies shuts himself off from other men, falsehood is therefore proscribed and, on a slightly lower level, murder and violence, which impose mutual silence. The mutual understanding and communication discovered by rebellion can only survive in the free exchange of dialogue. Every ambiguity, every mis-understanding, lead to death; clear language and simple words are the only salvation from it." And Camus observes in a footnote that "it is worth noting that the language peculiar to totalitarian doc-trines is always a scholastic or administrative language."[48]

Writing in his journal during World War II, Romanian novelist Mihail Sebastian comes close to Camus in his comments on what happens to language in times of war and crisis: "Later, much later, a study may be written about a strange phenomenon of these times: namely, the fact that words are losing their meaning, becoming weightless and devoid of content. Their speakers do not believe them, while their hearers do not understand them. If you analyzed word by word, grammatically, syntactically, and semantically, the declarations to be found almost daily in the newspapers, and if you opposed these with the facts to which they refer, you would see that there is an absolute split between word and reality."[49]

In her account of her own life and the lives of her grandmother and mother, Jung Chang examined how China, during the late 1950s, "slid into doublespeak. Words became divorced from reality, responsibility, and people's read thoughts. Lies were told with ease because words had lost their meanings—and had ceased to be taken seriously by others."[50]

Inflated language, a kind of euphemism, is another bar to clar-ity. Tocqueville once again gives a useful example. Social climbing will push people to "enhance a very coarse profession with a Greek or Latin name. The more the job is low and distant from science, the more the name is pompous and erudite. Thus it is that our rope dancers are transformed into acrobats and funambulists."[51]

Euphemisms are sometimes used to distance the speaker from other people. Torturers in Baghdad are reported to throw political prisoners into a tank of battery acid known as the "swimming pool."[52] Melvin Konner provides an extensive list of distancing slang that hospital residents and interns use, including "hang crepe" (given the condition of the patient, you will need to hang crepe when talking with the family to get them to expect the worst) and "crispy critter" (a child suffering from major burns). Konner suggests that if such language "seems frequently brutal and egotistical, we should consider the circumstances that produce it and remember that it is a revealing body of expression that may well be essential to their survival."[53]

Euphemisms sometimes serve appropriate social functions. If you have had to leave the table at a formal dinner party because of a stomach ailment, you would not want the host to describe in explicit terms the reasons for your abrupt departure. Or if you are an executive causing the abrupt departure of an employee, you might want to use language in the letter of termination that is clear but not necessarily brutally clear (as in, "Dear Joe. You're fired. Sincerely, Ruth"). With all the emphasis on clear language and short sentences, we would do well to consider situations where such an emphasis would be inappropriate. Richard Lanham's *Anti-Style: A Textbook* is a useful antidote in this regard.[54] Perhaps in the end we can go back to Orwell's advice: "What is above all needed is to let the meaning choose the word, and not the other way about. In prose, the worse thing one can do with words is to surrender to them."[55]

Sentence Structure, Order, and Syntax

"Rhetorical form is one of the carriers of meaning," Edward Corbett reminds us, and certainly the sentence (from the Latin, *sententia*, "a way of thinking") is one of those forms and carriers.[56]

More broadly, Richard Weaver helps us understand the implications of sentence structure choice in noting the differences
between the simple and the complex sentence:

> The complex sentence will be found nearly always to
> express some sort of hierarchy, whether spatial, moral, or
> causal, with its subordinate members describing the
> lower orders. In simple-sentence style we would write:
> "Tragedy began in Greece. It is the highest form of liter-
> ary art." There is no disputing that these sentences, in
> this sequence, could have a place in mature expression.
> But they do not have the same effect as "Tragedy, which
> is the highest form of literary art, began in Greece" or
> "Tragedy, which began in Greece, is the highest form of
> literary art." What has occurred is the critical process
> of subordination. The two ideas have been transferred
> from a conglomerate to an articulated unity, and the very
> fact of subordination makes inevitable the emergence of
> a focus of interest. Is our passage about the highest form
> of literary art or about the cultural history of Greece?
> The form of the complex sentence makes it unnecessary
> to waste any words in explicit assertion of that.[57]

Lord Chesterfield, by his own assessment an expert on pleasing
and persuading, advises his son on the strategies of sentence structure composition:

> I have spoken frequently in Parliament, and not always
> without some applause; and therefore I can assure you,
> from my experience, that there is very little in it. The
> elegancy of the style, and the turn of the periods, make
> the chief impression upon the hearers. Give them but
> one or two round and harmonious periods in a speech,

which they will retain and repeat; and they will go home as well satisfied, as people do from the Opera, humming all the way one or two favourite tunes that have struck their ears, and were easily caught. Most people have ears, but few have judgment; tickle those ears, and, depend upon it, you will catch their judgments, such as they are.[58]

Sir Arthur Quiller-Couch points out the necessity of clear order and good syntax:

> In writing, whether in prose or in verse, we can only produce our effect by a series of successive small impressions, dripping our meaning (so to speak) into the reader's mind—with the correspondent advantage, in point of vivacity, that our picture keeps moving all the while. Now obviously this throws a greater strain on his patience whom we address. Man at the best is a narrow-mouthed bottle. Through the conduit of speech he can utter— as you, my hearers, can receive—only one word at a time. In writing . . . you are as a commander filing out his battalion through a narrow gate that allows only one man at a time to pass; and your reader, as he receives the troops, has to reform and reconstruct them. No matter how large or how involved the subject, it can be communicated only in that way. You see, then, what an obligation we owe to him of order and arrangement; and why, apart from felicities and curiosities of diction, the old rhetoricians laid such stress upon order and arrangement as duties we owe to those to honour us with their attention.[59]

Abraham Lincoln, a master craftsman of prose, provides our final example of the importance of order and syntax:

There were many books in New Salem and few escaped
the inquiring and insatiable Lincoln, who read them, not
casually and in haste, but with infinite care and thoroughness, often writing out what he had read, to be sure
he understood. "I have," states a credible witness,
"known him to write a proposition in three different
forms in order to state the meaning as clearly and simply
as possible—and to spend half a day doing so."[60]

Delivery and Tone

Rhetoric has been given a bad name by those who suggest that the
discipline is primarily a bag of emotional tricks designed to fool an
audience. Given the emphasis in past centuries on the formal qualities of speech delivery and tone at what was seen as the demise of
content, philosophy, and ethics, the bad name may be in part
deserved. But we should not overlook the importance of delivery
and tone. They give us a sense of the speaker's attitude toward himself and also of the speaker's attitude toward the audience. Such
variables as "vocal pitch and quality, facial expression, and direct-
ness of eye contact" will tell us much.[61]

In *The Legal Imagination*, James Boyd White draws on Stark
Young's observations on tempo and tone in language:

> The tempo and tone are languages quite as the word is,
> sometimes one of the three is more important to the
> idea, sometimes another. The plain word *no* means sim-
> ply negation or refusal, but by tempo and vocal tone
> other meanings are added. When a character asks, Are
> you certain of his guilt? and another answers *no*, he is
> speaking two languages, one of the language of the
> word, which in this case remains the same; the other of
> music, by which the meaning can be changed at will. If
> he says *no* at once in a clear tone, *no* fifty seconds after
> the question and in a shrill tone, *no* one minute after

the question in an angry tone, and so on, he is plainly
saying different things, things of which the word is only
a small part. The gradations and values of sound in the
theatre are in their way as infinite and inexhaustible as
music is.[62]

We noted in Chapter Two that information seeking has political and, even more important, ethical implications. We note here
the same sentiment. The choice of terminology, the choice of
euphemism or clear language, the choice of sentence structure, the
choice of order and syntax, the choice of delivery and tone: all of
these choices carry ethical freight. All of us, and certainly leaders,
have much to consider in weighing our choices of how to speak.
These choices are ethical in another sense as well, in that persuasion is an ecological matter.

Ecology of Persuasion

The title of his 1972 book, *Steps to an Ecology of Mind,* gives us a
sense of one of Gregory Bateson's ways of viewing the world. There
are connections to be acknowledged and understood, Bateson
argued:

> There is an ecology of bad ideas, just as there is an ecol-
> ogy of weeds, and it is characteristic of the system that
> basic error propagates itself. It branches out like a rooted
> parasite through the tissues of life, and everything gets
> into a rather peculiar mess. When you narrow down your
> epistemology and act on the premise "What interests me
> is me, or my organization, or my species," you chop off
> consideration of other loops of the loop structure. You
> decide that you want to get rid of the by-products of
> human life and that Lake Erie will be a good place to put
> them. You forget that the eco-mental system called Lake

Erie is a part of *your* wider eco-mental system—and that
if Lake Erie is driven insane, its insanity is incorporated
in the larger system of *your* thought and experience.[63]

It is in this way, then, that Bateson considers the "problem of
how to transmit our ecological reasoning to those whom we wish to
influence in what seems to us to be an ecologically 'good' direction."
As Bateson concludes, "The means by which one man influences
another are part of the ecology of ideas in their relationship, and
part of the larger ecological system within which that relationship
exists."[64]

In *Rights Talk*, Mary Ann Glendon refers to the ten-second
sound bites that are preferred by the media but actually "constrict
opportunities for the sort of ongoing dialogue upon which a regime
of ordered liberty ultimately depends" (bumper sticker reasoning, as
I put it). She notes, "A tendency to frame nearly every social controversy in terms of a clash of rights (a woman's right to her own
body vs. a fetus's right to life) impedes compromise, mutual understanding, and the discovery of common ground. A penchant for absolute formulations ('I have the right to do whatever I want with
my property') promotes unrealistic expectations and ignores both
social costs and the rights of others. Saturated with rights, political
language can no longer perform the important function of facilitating public discussion of the right ordering of our lives together.
Just as rights exist for us only through being articulated, other goods
are not even available to be considered if they can be brought to
expression only with great difficulty, or not at all."[65]

Here Glendon is close to Michael Ignatieff: "Our needs are made
of words: they come to us in speech, and they can die for lack of expression. Without a public language to help us find our words, our
needs will dry up in silence."[66] And listening with approval to
Ignatieff is John Dewey: "Expression of ideas in communication is
one of the indispensable conditions of the awakening of thought
not only in others, but in ourselves. If ideas when aroused cannot

be communicated they either fade away or become warped and mor-
bid."[67] Speech can prevent thought, and thus further speech, as
Orwell reminds us: "The purpose of Newspeak was not only to provide a medium of expression for the world-view and mental habits
proper to the devotees of Ingsoc, but to make all other modes of
thought impossible."[68]

Glendon goes on to say that "when political actors resort to slo-
gans and images rather than information and explanations, they
hinder the exercise of citizenship. Leaving so much unsaid, they create a discrepancy between what we officially proclaim and what we
need in order to make sense of our lives."[69]

In a penetrating essay on obscure writing, Primo Levi suggests a
larger ecological relationship: "He who does not know how to communicate, or communicates badly, in a code that belongs only to him
or a few others, is unhappy, and spreads unhappiness around him."
Levi goes on to say that someone who engages in bad communication deliberately "is wicked or at least a discourteous person, because
he imposes labor, anguish, or boredom on his readers."[70]

Richard Weaver notes that rhetoric "supplies the bonds of community, for community rests upon informed sentiment."[71] If this is
so, then bad speaking means ill-informed sentiment that threatens
the existence of community.

Words uttered can have an immediate impact, even without
apparent intent. Is there no one who will rid me of this troublesome
priest? asks Henry II, and before too much later, Becket is murdered
in the cathedral at Canterbury. And the impact surely can go
beyond the immediate to the larger surround. Robert Kennedy had
a sense of the impact of words on the larger surround when he dis-
couraged his aides from speaking harshly of Lyndon Johnson.
Kennedy disliked and distrusted Johnson, to be sure. But he did not
like the harsh attacks and would not contribute to that kind of talk.
"A clash of personalities would undermine the senator's policy arguments and cheapen his public stature. And it would weaken the
presidency, an office Kennedy expected, someday, to occupy."[72]

Michel Berenbaum, Georgetown University theology professor, reminds us that "a natural expansion of verbal violence is physical violence." Berenbaum was reported as convinced that some of the "unconscionable verbal violence in Israel was a factor in the deranged actions of the Rabin assassination and worries about some of the same patterns in America."[73]

Rollo May quotes W. H. Auden: "As a poet, there is only one political duty, and that is to defend one's language from corruption. And this is particularly serious now. It's being so quickly corrupted. When it's corrupted, people lose faith in what they hear, and this leads to violence."[74]

In *The Federalist* No. 1, Alexander Hamilton spoke with "candour" on the necessity of moderate speech, holding out the hope of reasoned discourse. He acknowledged that bad judgment can come from numerous causes and that we can "see wise and good men on the wrong as well as on the right side of question." Moreover, he suggested, "we are not always sure, that those who advocate the truth are influenced by purer principles than their antagonists." And, finally, he saw as ill judged "that intolerant spirit, which has, at all times, characterised political parties. For, in politics, as in religion, it is equally absurd to aim at making proselytes by fire and sword. Heresies in either can rarely be cured by persecution."[75]

There is not enough space here to begin to document the negative political campaign advertisements—the attack ads that show just how far we are from essays that compose *The Federalist*. But I will offer one further example of the results emerging from what is seen as do-what-it-takes-to-get-elected rhetoric.

Riding the term limits bandwagon in 1992, Washington State politician George Nethercutt unseated House Speaker Thomas Foley. Nethercutt promised to serve but three terms. However, after his three terms, Nethercutt found it advantageous to run again. For reasons that may be difficult to fathom, his constituents returned him to the House for a fourth term. (Perhaps several decades from now, Nethercutt will be defeated by yet another "term limits" cam-

paigner.) My point here is that despite his reelection, the congress-
man has in some way contributed to the overall decline in respect
for politicians and the political process. The lesson many young
people learn from hearing speech that can so easily reverse itself
(war is peace, freedom is slavery, term limits are essential, term limits are meaningless) is that, once again, words either lose their
meaning or simply do not matter. In a society where people can use
words to mean whatever they want them to mean, words are simply weapons to be used to gain an immediate advantage.

"He broke a campaign pledge. And not just any pledge, but the
one that defined him. And he has broken it in spectacularly
appalling fashion, reinforcing the idea that politicians are a bunch
of dishonorable crumbs only out for themselves." "'A lot of people
will do or say anything to get elected,' [former Colorado Senator
William] Armstrong says. 'That cynicism is a cancer on the body
politic. And any time a guy like Nethercutt can get away with a
stunt like this it's just bad.'"[76]

I already noted the debilitating results of some arguments from
consequence, with the examples of how to promote arts in the
schools and how to argue for school desegregation. To argue that
either should be linked to a rise in achievement test scores is to give
away a great deal, and not only in terms of the particular program
in question. Once arts proponents start arguing from consequence,
with all sorts of what turn out to be strained attempts to link arts
and test scores, the arguments will take on a life of their own, a
legitimacy. These arguments will become accepted as the way to
make the case to the district. Music programs will be justified on the
basis of increased test scores, as will additional programs in creative
writing and every other "soft" educational offering. The ecological
connection of the arguments cannot be denied once established,
and the more it is used on one situation, the more it will be used in
other situations, building on itself and providing its own justification. It is curious that it matters little if the modest arts program is
actually adopted. Once the argument from consequence is made and

accepted, others with other programs to propose will have to follow the form.

Persuasion and the Ecology (and Ethics) of Response

So far we have been talking about the ethics of persuasion from the point of view of the person attempting to persuade. But persuasion is never unidirectional. The persuader is trying to persuade an audience, and as a member of the audience, we have choices to make. We can choose to accept the claims and how those claims are made. Or we can choose to reject those claims or the basis on which they are made. With these kinds of choices, we are on ethical ground.

For example, at a school staff meeting, a teacher repeatedly argues that some students, especially those from poor families, lack the basic intelligence to do the work. "We all know that they are dumb," she says. You are at that staff meeting. You have to decide whether to reinforce the expressed stereotype (and you can reinforce by either vocalizing your support or remaining silent) or to contradict what the teacher is saying.

When a speaker uses euphemisms that obscure meaning, you must choose to accept the language or ask for clarification. When a speaker uses hurtful language (hurtful to those present or hurtful regardless of who is in the audience), you must choose to speak out against such language or to let the language ride and thus by default support the usage.

A speaker uses passive voice to disclaim responsibility: "Mistakes were made." You can choose to accept or reject, reinforce or deny.

Conclusion

As a leader, you will set the tone of an organization not only by your own speech but by how you choose to accept or reject the speech of others. If you are expedient in how you respond to the speech of others, you will show yourself as expedient.

Clearly the question of how to respond has ecological dimensions. Others in a given organization are always watching their leaders with care, looking for probabilities of future behavior. If you are expedient in one situation, the odds are that you will be expedient in another. Moreover, your giving expediency your blessing tells everyone in the organization that they too can be expedient in how they choose to respond to the speech of others—and can be expedient in how they choose to speak themselves in trying to persuade others. Gregory Bateson suggests that it is a characteristic of error to propagate itself in a system. And in a similar manner, it is a characteristic of responses to speeches to propagate and spread.

We can see, then, that the ethics of persuasion and the ecology of persuasion pose political and ethical dilemmas for leaders. And perhaps we can see, with Ben Jonson, that "language most shows a man: speak, that I may see thee. It springs out of the most retired, and inmost parts of us, and is the image of the parent of it, the mind. No glass renders a man's form or likeness, so true as his speech."[77]

4

The Political Context
of Leadership

We have up to this point been talking about leadership as constituting a language of persuasion, about information seeking, and about the ethics and ecology of persuasion. We have been talking about these matters without specific reference to the political context in which leadership takes place. But there is always a political context, and the conduct of leadership interacts in all sorts of ways with that context. Surely, we can argue, public leaders by definition are leaders within the political context and mold and are molded by that context. We can argue too that educational leaders interact with the political context. And in very general terms, private sector leaders can be seen to interact with the political context. Even those arguing for virtually unregulated capitalism will acknowledge that there are laws to be made, laws to be obeyed; regulatory agencies to be consulted, dominated, followed, or ignored.

But political contexts range from relatively free and open civic cultures that have liberal constitutional democracies to despotic cultures that are relatively unfree and unopen, and nondemocratic. Given that leadership does occur in and with a political context and given that there are different kinds of political contexts, we need to ask two questions:

1. Are there any differences between leadership in a civic culture with free and open democracy and leadership in a despotic culture?

2. If there are differences, do those differences obtain just
   in public leadership positions, or do they obtain in private
   sector leadership positions as well?

To develop responses to these questions, let us look first at some
elements that differentiate a despotic culture characterized by
oppression, relatively little participation, and relatively little freedom, and a civic culture characterized by a liberal democracy in a
free society. In trying to so differentiate, we are looking at general
features, general indicators; we are not talking about totally pure
cultures or states. And although some features of one culture might
arguably be found in the other, there are enough differences to be
able to make useful distinctions. As Hamlet says, "I know a hawk
from a handsaw."

Robert Conquest notes differences between "civic" culture and
"despotic" culture in this way: "In the 'civic' culture, the polity is
articulated and decisions are made (in principle at least) in accor-
dance with a balance of interests, through consultation with and
acceptance by the various sections of the community; while in the
'despotic' culture, the decisions are taken by a single man or a single
group and the population is merely a passive element."[1]

Conquest goes on to suggest that to speak of a civic culture is to
give us a "basis on which improvements can be made. For a civic
society is a society in which the various elements can express themselves politically, in which an articulation exists between these elements at the political level: not a perfect social order, which is in
any case unobtainable, but a society that hears, considers and
reforms grievances. It is not necessarily democratic, but it contains
the possibility of democracy."[2]

Herbert Muller argued that the best society is one that would
lead to "being a free, responsible individual with a mind of one's
own." It is, he said, following Karl Popper, an open society, "an
adventurous society that has broken with the universal, prehistoric
custom of regarding ancient customs as magical or sacred, that views

its institutions as man-made for human purposes and examines their suitability for these purposes, that welcomes variety and change instead of enforcing rigid conformity, and that accordingly provides its members with personal opportunities and responsibilities beyond mere obedience. It is Athens as opposed to Sparta."[3]

We can get another sense of the distinctions between civic and despotic culture by considering some of the features of democracy offered by Robert Dahl:

1. Elected officials. Control over government decisions about policy is constitutionally vested in elected officials.
2. Free and fair elections. Elected officials are chosen in frequent and fairly conducted elections in which coercion is comparatively uncommon.
3. Inclusive suffrage. Practically all adults have the right to vote in the election of officials.
4. Right to run for office. Practically all adults have the right to run for elective offices in the government, though age limits may be higher for holding office than for the suffrage.
5. Freedom of expression. Citizens have a right to express themselves without danger of severe punishment on political matters broadly defined, including criticism of officials, the government, the regime, the socioeconomic order, and the prevailing ideology.
6. Alternative information. Citizens have a right to seek out alternative sources of information. Moreover, alternative sources of information exist and are protected by laws.
7. Associational autonomy. To achieve their various rights, including those listed above, citizens also have a right to form relatively independent

associations or organizations, including independent political parties and interest groups.[4]

With these elements in mind, we can make basic distinctions
between despotic and civic cultures. One way to begin to make such
distinctions is to consider the Freedom House surveys of freedom
around the world. For close to fifty years, the Freedom House has
examined the conditions of freedom in the world's countries, looking at both political rights (the ability to "form political parties that
represent a significant range of voter choice and whose leaders can
openly compete for and be elected to positions of power in government") and civil liberties (upheld by respecting and protecting citizens' religious, ethnic, economic, linguistic, and other rights,
including gender and family rights, personal freedoms, and freedoms
of press, belief, and association).[5]

The 1999–2000 Freedom House survey of 192 countries finds
85 countries that can be considered free, 59 partly free, and 48 not
free in terms of political rights and civil liberties.[6] It is difficult to
disagree with the findings of the survey. We can consider such countries as Afghanistan, North Korea, Algeria, and Iraq as despotic and
not free, and we can, I trust, find civic cultures in countries such as
the United States, Canada, Germany, Australia, and Sweden.
Again, we are looking at basic differences here, and not considering ideal, pure types; we are recognizing too that while a country
may be basically unfree, some in that country may be able to exercise a modicum of freedom, and in free countries, some people experience less freedom than others. By a basic comparison, however,
we can get some sense of the "institutions, procedures, and habits
of mind that go to make a political regime actual."[7] That is, we can
discern what happens to people in a despotic culture or a civic culture. And we can get some sense of how people are motivated to
behave in a despotic culture as compared with a civic culture.
Again, with Hamlet, we can know a hawk from a handsaw.[8]

The World of Despotic Culture

As a general rule, when trying to understand the interplay of culture and politics and behavior, useful guidance can be found by consulting Alexis de Tocqueville. At the conclusion of Volume One of his *Democracy in America*, we find the oft-quoted and still useful distinction between behavior and motivation in a despotic culture and in a civic culture:

> The American struggles against the obstacles that nature opposes to him; the Russian grapples with men. The one combats the wilderness and barbarism, the other, civilization vested with all its arms; thus the conquests of the Americans are made with the plowshare of the laborer; those of the Russian, with the sword of the soldier.
>
> To attain his goal, the first relies on personal interest and allows the force and reason of individuals to act, without directing them.
>
> The second in a way concentrates all the power of society in one man.
>
> The one has freedom for his principal means of action; the other servitude.
>
> Their point of departure is different, their ways are diverse; nonetheless, each of them seems called by a secret design of Providence to hold the destinies of half the world in its hands one day.[9]

Tocqueville, a French aristocrat, had headed to the United States in 1831 to get his own sense of this new nation, democracy, and equality. Later in the same decade, another French aristocrat, marquis de Custine, headed literally and figuratively in the opposite direction, to Russia. His findings resulting from the journey have been questioned by some, but Custine seems close to the mark (and close to Tocqueville) in his basic observations and conclusions about the despotic state of Russia.[10] Custine suggests that "all Russians and all who wish to live in Russia impose on themselves unconditional silence. Here, nothing is said, but everything is known. Secret conversations should be very interesting; but who permits himself to indulge in them? To think, to discern, is to become suspect."[11] Thus, he says, "only silence and fear reign." There is, he observes, little inquiry, little organized action, few assemblies, peaceable or otherwise: "There are no great throngs in Russia. . . . That is the advantage of a country where there is no nation. The first time there is a crowd in Petersburg, the city will be crushed. In a society organized as this one is, a crowd would mean a revolution."[12] (And here Custine's observation reminds us of the Falun Gong demonstrations in Beijing, with ten thousand people coming out of nowhere with no warning, gathering outside party headquarters, with the Communist party frantically trying to stop what it saw—and continues to see—as a serious threat to its existence.)[13] It is fear, silence, and lying that Custine returns to as the basic behaviors that he observes in despotic Russia:

> It must be said that the Russians of all classes conspire with miraculous harmony to make duplicity prevail in their country. They have a dexterity in lying, a naturalness in falsehood, the success of which is as revolting to my candor as it is appalling to me. . . . Everything that gives a meaning and a goal to political institutions reduces itself here to one lone sentiment—fear. In Russia, fear replaces, that is to say paralyzes, thought; this sentiment, when it alone reigns, can produce only the appearance of civilization; though not sunned by short-sighted legislators, fear can never be the soul of a well-organized society; it is not order—it is only the veil over chaos. . . . Where liberty is lacking, soul and truth are lacking.[14]

What Custine saw in Russia he could have as easily seen one hundred years later, with a despotic culture turning into a totalitarian regime following the Russian Revolution. Assuming Custine could have even made it across the border, he would have found Lenin laying the foundation of the terror that would continued almost unlimited under Stalin.[15]

And when Custine talks about labeling political opponents as mentally ill, he is horrifyingly current. A theologian wrote with favor about the Catholic church. Instead of throwing him in jail, the emperor had in mind a worse sentence: "The man was not a criminal to be punished, but a madman to be locked up. . . . The sick man would be turned over to the care of doctors," and after three years of this "new form of torture," the theologian was ready to declare himself "insane."[16]

Custine could have been describing a typical means of torture used by the Soviet police to attempt to control dissidents. Joseph Brodsky, who was later awarded the Nobel Prize for literature, spent years in a "psychiatric hospital" being injected with drugs that caused intense pain with the slightest movement of his body.[17]

That kind of despotism, lack of freedom, and disregard for human life are hardly limited to the Bolshevik regime, of course. We can find similar instances in Nazi Germany, China under Mao and beyond, Cambodia under the Khmer Rouge and Pol Pot: the depressing list goes on and on.[18] It is a list we should pay considerable attention to, although there are many who seem to have forgotten these and many other terrors—or prefer to pretend they never knew, or if they did, much worse was happening in the United States.

In Russia, the troubles continue. "The courts almost completely fail in their role as the ultimate safeguard of freedom and order," one observer notes, putting the blame not only on the rulers but on "public attitudes and behaviour": "First, Russians themselves, quite understandably, think that many of their laws are bad and feel no compunction about breaking them. Second, they have little faith in formal ways of complaining. As a result, they never use them. 'We have no tradition of living by the law,' says [human rights leader Ludmila] Alexeyeva. 'Faced with a problem, people try bribes, personal connections, or force.' After decades of totalitarianism and centuries of autocracy, it would be silly to expect Russia to sprout a strong civil society and independent institutions like mushrooms."[19]

What we might expect in Russia—and in similar situations elsewhere—is reflected in the following observation in the *Tao Te Ching*: "When government is harsh, people respond with cunning."[20] Sometimes the best response is to be invisible. Writing in Cairo in 1299–1300, a commentator cites a caliph as saying, "The best life has he who has an ample house, a beautiful wife, and sufficient means, who does not know us and whom we do not know."[21]

In addition to cunning and invisibility, many people respond to the repressive nature of despotic cultures with fear, submission, and compliance. In "The Bronze Horseman," one of the most famous poems to emerge from Russia, Pushkin tells of St. Petersburg, the great statue of Peter the Great astride his horse, the great flood of 1824, and Evgeny, a poor young man in love. The devastating flood sweeps away his beloved. Maddened with grief, Evgeny approaches the statue, telling Peter that he is to blame for what has happened: "Up there, great wonder-worker you, beware!" He races away, only to be chased through the city by the Bronze Horseman. From then on, whenever Evgeny by chance comes to the great square, he raises his worn-out cap, averts his eyes, and slinks away. This most intriguing poem has been interpreted variously (like any other complex work of art), but the notion of maddened risk taking in questioning authority followed by submission in response to threat is one given us with great clarity.[22]

In an interesting study of everyday behavior of people in the Soviet regime of the 1930s, Sheila Fitzpatrick notes that people were frightened of the regime, "given the regime's proven willingness to punish, the strength of its punitive arm, its long and vengeful memory, and the predictability of its outbursts." The response of citizens "was passive conformity and outward obedience. This did not mean, however, that the Soviet citizens necessarily had a high respect for authority. On the contrary, a degree of skepticism, even a refusal to take the regime's most serious pronouncements seriously, was the norm."[23] (When an authoritarian regime is about to fall, compliance lessens considerably, as reflected in the story of the Polish Solidarity guests visiting Vaclav Havel and his wife just prior to the fall of the Czech regime. After dinner, "Havel had a flash of inspiration: instead of using the bathroom, he led his guests outside to urinate in full view of the secret-police surveillance cameras he knew were routinely deployed in a cottage opposite his house. . . . A police state that prompted such open mockery was already deprived of its most potent weapon, the ability to inspire fear, and its fate was all but sealed.")[24]

An appearance of obedience is not found solely in despotic cultures, of course. From time to time, many of us find it prudent to accede to demands made by others in the organization, figuring that, like the Soviet citizens described by Fitzpatrick, "this, too, shall pass." One chooses one's battles and conserves one's strength. But the stakes are considerably higher in a despotic regime than in most organizations in a democratic civic culture. In a democratic civil culture, I might be ostracized for a time or not get promoted as fast if my underlying lack of commitment to the organization is unmasked, but I probably will not be shot.

Compliance behavior is common in despotic cultures. Suspicion is another behavior that tinctures the whole, along with caution and unwillingness to express criticism or dissent. Sergei Eisenstein's subtle movie *Ivan the Terrible* was to have had three parts. The third part was never made because of the opposition from Stalin, focused on the increasing suspicions among Ivan's newly created palace guard. An early supporter of Ivan, one who gives his son to Ivan as one of the first members of the palace guard, falls under suspicion and is killed—by his own son. Once suspicion is afoot, it is difficult to counter it. In Shakespeare's *Richard II,* the deposed king says to the duke of Northumberland, in effect, "Henry knows you helped him overthrow me. What is to prevent him thinking you're going to overthrow him too?"[25] Suspicion tinctured East Germany until the collapse of the Soviet empire. The regime might not have been as terror oriented as the Soviet Union, but the secret police and their spies were legion.[26]

The world of despotic culture is bleak—too bleak, perhaps, for some who might say the emphasis is skewed toward a negative and unoptimistic view. The emphasis on tyranny and despotism is justified, I think, in looking at the history of the world. Perhaps Francis Fukuyama is on to something with his notion of the "end of history," suggesting that nations ultimately end up with a liberal political democracy. But as Jean-François Revel pointed out, "It is all very well to dismiss a residual or recrudescent totalitarianism as a 'rear-guard action,' but we should not forget that our lives are lived from one rear-guard action to another. Indeed, entire generations have consumed their existence in these allegedly marginal battles. Laid end to end, both in space and time, they have involved the majority of this planet's population and most of this century."[27] Tyranny and despotism and oppression have not yet run their course, as the Freedom House surveys remind those who wish to see and hear.

The World of Democratic Civic Culture

To move from the world of despotic culture to the world of democratic civic culture is to move to the light of day, the freshness of reasoned discourse, and the welcome exchange of information. The importance of open exchange in a democratic civic society has long been recognized. In his Funeral Oration, Pericles takes care to note:

> We throw open our city to the world, and never by alien
> acts exclude foreigners from any opportunity of learning
> or observing, although the eyes of an enemy may occa-

sionally profit by our liberality; trusting less in system and policy than to the native spirit of our citizens. . . . Our public men have, besides politics, their private affairs to attend to, and our ordinary citizens, though occupied with the pursuits of industry, are still fair judges of public matters; for, unlike any other nation, we regard the citizen who takes no part in these duties not as unambitious but useless, and we are able to judge proposals even if we cannot originate them; instead of looking on discussion as a stumbling-block in the way of action, we think it an indispensable preliminary to any wise action at all.[28]

In the United States, open exchange of information has been a critical element in the development of a free society. As we know, Tocqueville headed west to the United States and found much to admire. Certainly he found much more freedom and openness than did Custine in Russia. The United States was not (and is not) perfect. Then, as now, there were needs for improvement, and there were, as there continue to be, threats to freedom and an open society. But despite the problems he discerned, Tocqueville found that the Americans were onto something. He notes, for example, the astonishing extent of information exchange, as shown in his discussion of rural Tennessee:

You see few churches, no schools; society, like the individual, seems to provide for nothing. . . . And yet, it's not quite a rustic society. Their customs have none of the *naiveté* of the fields; the philosophical and argumentative spirit of the English crops up there as in all parts of America; and there is an astonishing circulation of letters and newspapers in the midst of these wild forests. We were traveling with the mail. From time to time we stopped before what they called the post. It was almost always an isolated house in the depth of the woods. There we dropped a large packet, from which doubtless each inhabitant of the neighbourhood came to take his share. I don't believe that in the most enlightened rural district in France there is carried on an intellectual exchange as rapid or as large as in these wildernesses.[29]

It was this sort of information provision and exchange that helped establish and legitimate the Republic. Daniel Boorstin notes that some eighty newspapers were published in the colonies at the time, and within twenty days after the adjournment of the Constitutional Convention, at least fifty-five had printed the full text of the draft Constitution.[30] The essays composing *The Federalist* and the *Anti-Federalist* provide further evidence of the openness of information and discussion, as do hundreds of other speeches, pamphlets, articles, broadsides, sermons, and letters of the time (materials that are worth more than a glance, particularly at a time when we might want to reflect on the low level of political discourse in our own time).[31]

In addition, in a democratic civic society, one finds free and open travel and an absence of fear. Self-interest rather than compliance is the norm. There is a free press, even when that press is seen as an irritant.[32] It should be noted too that even in a democratic civic society, there are temptations to use governmental powers to silence opponents, as for example, the Sedition Act passed by the Federalists to shut out the opposition.[33] Eternal vigilance as the price of liberty does not apply only to watchfulness against external threats.

Furthermore, we can expect to find in a democratic civic society attention to due process of law—the kind of due process Clarence speaks of in *Richard III* in remonstrating those who have come to murder him:

> Are you drawn forth from a world of men
> To slay the innocent? What is my offence?

Where is the evidence that doth accuse me?
What lawful quest have giv'n their verdict up
Unto the frowning judge: Or who pronounc'd
The bitter sentence of poor Clarence' death?
Before I be convict by course of law,
To threaten me with death is most unlawful.[34]

Leadership in Despotic and Civic Cultures

There are basic differences, then, between despotic and civic cultures and differences between the behaviors, norms, and motivations of people in the two cultures. We can find three (at the very least) differences: (1) passive acceptance versus outward skepticism, (2) silence versus outspoken criticism, and (3) compliance versus consent. Given these differences, it is reasonable to assume that leadership in a despotic culture is necessarily different from leadership in a civic culture. Such an assumption seems prima facie obvious for public leaders. The focus for public leaders in a despotic society is on compliance with top-down directives and checking up on people. There is little need to worry about building consensus because the state is so powerful that no real opposition can be mounted. Nor is there any real need to worry about maintaining one's legitimacy as a public leader because, again, the state is so powerful that legitimacy cannot be effectively (and publicly) questioned. Thus, a leader in a despotic culture can make the kind of moves Lenin often made. Consider, for example, Lenin's memo of August 11, 1918: "Comrades! The uprising of the five kulak districts should be *mercilessly* suppressed. The interests of the *entire* revolution requires this. . . . Hang (hang without fail, so *the people see*) *no fewer than one hundred* known kulaks, rich men, bloodsuckers . . . take from them *all* the grain." Lenin, ever the careful controller of evil, concludes with a postscript telling how to staff the operation: "Find some truly hard people."[35] It would be difficult for a leader in a civic culture to act in this way.

By contrast, in a civic society, public leaders are more likely to focus on persuasion, consensus building, and maintaining legitimacy. Public leaders can be voted into office and voted out of office, and thus it is important for them to pay close attention to what the public is trying to say. Public leaders in a civic society are likely to spend much more time seeking ways to adjudicate conflicts of interest (as in not-in-my-backyard disputes) and seeking ways to ensure that the voices of various interest groups (including those often silent or on the margins) are given a fair hearing. Even under conditions of war, we can find public leaders proceeding with consensus building. The consensus-building strategies vary, of course. Franklin Roosevelt tended to seek advice from a few aides rather than formal bodies or experts. Churchill, on the other hand, "reported to his War Cabinet every day on his activities; he consulted his assembled chiefs of staff regularly; he reported periodically to Parliament; and he drew constantly on the permanent secretariat. . . . He would not sign the Atlantic Charter aboard the battleship off Nova Scotia until its full text had been cabled to the War Cabinet and a reply received."[36]

There are differences that will necessarily obtain for educational leaders. In a despotic society, educational leaders will operate as bureaucrats who fully understand that their role is to produce students who will follow orders without question. Schools must employ (and supervise closely) teachers who will follow orders without question in teaching materials and ideas as specified by the state and in administering without question whatever tests the state deems necessary. By contrast, educational leaders in a democratic civic society might be expected to adjudicate conflicts of interest between various groups of parents and the state. Moreover, such educational leaders might see themselves as facilitating gatherings of education professionals who collectively, and with parents and community members, will devise and provide educational experiences geared to meet the needs of students rather than solely meet the expressed (or perceived) needs of the state bureaucracy.

There are differences that will obtain for private sector leaders as well. In a despotic society, there usually is not much of a private sector other than a nonlegitimate black market or some version of the Russian mafia. To the extent that there is at least a partial private sector, its leaders will tend to be more interested in establishing working (if not necessarily lawful) relationships with state bureaucrats. By contrast, private sector leaders in a democratic civic society are free to focus on persuading customers, the government, and the public; they are bound not by fear or compliance but by the market, the laws, and their creativity.

These are some of the basic differences between being a leader (public, educational, private sector) in a despotic culture and in a democratic civic culture. There are additional differences that we need to consider as well. In Chapter Two, we outlined the role of a leader as seeker of information. Is information seeking different in despotic cultures and democratic civic cultures? Clearly, yes. Only in a civic culture with freedom and openness will one be able to seek information freely and without fear. Leaders need to behave in a lawful manner when they seek information in a civic culture. They cannot use torture. Note, again, that we are dealing with an ecological question as well. If you use torture to seek information, you are not only in the wrong ethically; you are threatening a free and open society.

Information seeking in a despotic society is made more difficult because of how much there is to hide. The penultimate scene in Part II of *Faust* has Mephistopheles, on orders from Faust, removing an old couple from their home. Resisting their fate, the couple is murdered. The scene is entitled, appropriately enough, "Dead of Night." It is always in the dead of night, when the lights of inquiry are dimmed, that oppressors make their moves. Thus, when King Leopold was plundering the Congo, his minions tried as much as possible to keep hidden the incredible outrages. Others, including Mark Twain, tried to call the world's attention to the brutalities. In Twain's *King Leopold's Soliloquy*, we hear Leopold complaining about the "trivial little kodak . . . the only witness I have encountered in my long experience that I couldn't bribe."[37]

Furthermore, public leaders in a despotic society can attempt to keep vital information from the public (and they usually succeed). They can follow the basic approach taken by Jean-Paul Sartre. Sartre did not want to change positions on the Bolshevik terror and the camps because to change positions (and acknowledge the terror) would confuse the French worker. In a despotic culture (or among those who appear to support despotic cultures), you can assume that the masses cannot or should not think and need to be told what to do and how to think.[38]

Moreover, in a despotic society, you will seek information to further a limited range of views. Leaders in despotic cultures tend to want not curious information seekers as part of their retinue. They prefer toadies.

In Chapter Three, we discussed the choices one makes when trying to persuade others. In a despotic culture, the choices of argument are limited. It is difficult to imagine a member of the Politburo suggesting to Stalin that they consider options contrary to what Stalin had just advocated. Consider, for example, Stalin's favorite slogan in the 1930s: "Life has become better, comrades, life has become more cheerful."[39] There were few who would have wanted to suggest to Stalin that life had become much, much worse.

We can then consider leadership differences in despotic and democratic civic cultures in terms of compliance versus consensus building, and in terms of top-down directives to be followed without question versus collaborative inquiry and dialogues between interest groups. Furthermore, we can consider leadership differences in terms of information seeking and choices of means of persuasion. These are important differences. But there are other important differences as well—differences that cut very deeply—and it is to these that we must now turn.

In Chapter One, we presented the basic function of leadership as constituting a language of persuasion and creating a persuaded audience. But it is clear by now that we have to move beyond defining good leadership as effective persuasion. A lynch mob can be a persuaded audience. The Nuremberg rallies in Nazi Germany were attended by persuaded audiences. But what of that? What we must conclude is that in a democratic civic society, merely creating a persuaded audience does not provide solid ethical and political grounding. There is a larger objective we must have in mind, one suggested by Ralph Lerner in his consideration of Edmund Burke, Abraham Lincoln, and Tocqueville: "Politicians of their rank have in view not only a persuaded audience but a more thoughtful public. Especially singular and noteworthy is the manner in which they undertake to make their public rise in some sense above itself."[40]

There are differences between "persuaded" and "more thoughtful," as well as differences between "audience" and "public." An audience in this sense can be seen as a passive recipient of the message of persuasion, whereas a public, particularly one "more thoughtful," gives us a sense of an aware community, active and alert and more than willing and able to look into things and askance at things. A thoughtful public is careful, contemplative, aware of its rights and responsibilities, willing to think about matters with a view to the future as well as the present, and willing to consider issues and proposed actions in relation to other issues and actions, as well how those issues and proposed actions bear on the fundamental moral and political grounding of the whole. In this sense of the public, as Lerner notes, "the conduct of the public's business demands enlarged views both from the few charged with that business and from the many empowered to select them. An electorate that expects its representatives to behave like lapdogs will get what it deserves—creeping servility—not what it most needs."[41]

A thoughtful public is difficult to sustain. When things are going well, it is easy to become slothful and unaware of our responsibilities for self-government. When we are under stress with many complicated variables and much uncertainty impinging on the polity, it is easy to oversimplify or to adopt the big project that will help us pretend that nothing has changed. It was this kind of big project that Tocqueville adverted to when he suggested that England and France should not compensate for national malaise "by making railroads."[42] It is also easy under such circumstances to succumb to demagoguery.

There is not much of a chance of having a thoughtful public in a despotic culture. A thoughtful public, one that values and practices open conversation, contention, and inquiry without having to hew to a party line, cannot emerge, let alone survive, under despotism. A thoughtful public requires a democratic civic culture in which to thrive. But it is only a more thoughtful public that can sustain that civic culture in the first place. All leaders—public, school, and private sector—have a double obligation here: to behave in their formal roles and as community members in ways that will encourage the growth and sustenance of the institutions and processes that are part of a democratic civic society, and at the same time, they must behave, again in their formal roles and as community members, in ways that model the behaviors and habits of mind associated with a more thoughtful public.

Leadership and the Conditions for Democracy

Creating and sustaining a more thoughtful public is a necessary condition for a democratic civic society. Are there other conditions that must be in place as well, conditions that must accompany a democratic civil society? If so, what might they be? And what bearing do these conditions have on the conduct of leadership?

Before considering these conditions for a democracy, we need to note that there are at least three relevant ways here to talk about conditions. In the first sense, we need to talk about conditions as prerequisites, as necessary elements. For example, we might want to argue that free and open inquiry is a condition for democracy, that is, a necessary element of democracy. Assuming we say it is a condition, then we can consider free and open inquiry in its ideal sense. In the best of all possible worlds, what would free and open inquiry look like? And then we can consider, following along the lines of the old folk song, what condition the condition is in: What currently is the state or condition of free and open inquiry? Do we have it? To what extent? Among all parts of the community? Or just some?

It is important to make the distinctions among the three ways of considering conditions. If we do not make the distinctions, we are likely to have conversations that end up in a dead end: I will be saying that free and open inquiry is a condition for democracy, someone else will be saying we do not have any real free and open inquiry, and the conversation will not be joined.

With these distinctions in mind, let us turn to eleven additional hypothesized conditions necessary for democracy:[43]

1. *Trust.* If there is no trust, people will not be able to enter into the kinds of long-term relationships necessary for political and social interaction in a democracy.[44]

2. *Exchange.* People must be able to exchange goods and services in order to survive in a democracy. The act of exchange is a way of building and sustaining relationships.[45]

3. *Social capital.* People have to have the social and political skills necessary to work together to understand problems and create solutions as opposed to simply accepting orders.[46] Social capital seems to work within the bounds of the "Matthew effect," with the rich getting richer. Thus, a difficulty in a democracy is how to secure and sustain social capital for all rather than for a select few.

4. *Respect for equal justice under law.* If there is no justice, we have no recourse other than self-interest, which is ultimately self-defeating.[47]

5. *Respect for civil discourse.* If people cannot talk to each other, advance ideas, adduce evidence, and weigh and consider without resorting to physical or verbal violence, it will be difficult for democracy to survive.[48]

6. *Recognition of the need for e pluribus unum.* The American democracy is not experienced simply by isolated groups, each celebrating its own peculiar identity. There must be some sort of glue that holds the whole together. But there must also be respect for individual and group differences. The trick here is to acknowledge and deal with the constant tension between the unum and the pluribus.

7. *Free and open inquiry.* This condition is central to a democracy. People will not be able to participate in any thoughtful way in a democracy unless they have the ability and inclination to inquire into all aspects of the workings of society.[49]

8. *Knowledge of rights.* If we do not know what our rights are, we will have difficulty exercising them. A people without knowledge of its rights can hardly be seen to participate effectively in a democracy.[50]

9. *Freedom.* As many have said, you have to have the power to exercise freedom and the insight to value it. Both conditions are necessary.[51] Robert Nisbet suggests that freedom is a "virtue only when there goes with it personal privacy, autonomy in some degree, and creativeness to the limit of one's faculties. . . . Democratic absolutism, chiefly in the manifestation of the thick, heavy bureaucracies we build today, can be as oppressive to the creative instinct, the curiosity itch, and the drive to explore as anything that exists more blatantly in the totalitarian state."[52]

10. *Recognition of the tension between freedom and order.* As Leo Strauss reminds us, we have to deal with the "freedom that is not license and the order that is not oppression."[53] If we maximize freedom and ignore order, we end up with anarchy. But if in our desire for order, we move beyond reasonable order to oppression, then we are no better off. The tension between freedom and order is a constant.

11. *Ecological understanding.*[54] The unit of survival is organism plus environment: the organism that destroys its environment

destroys itself. The only way for democracy to survive is for the larger environment to survive.

If these conditions are necessary and if conditions are created by people rather than by a deus ex machina or magic or the Tooth Fairy, then we can assume that leaders of people have an important role in creating and sustaining these conditions. If leaders are seen as violating trust (as, for example, with the politician described in the last part of Chapter Three), then that condition will surely be threatened. If school leaders refuse to allow free and open inquiry in schools because of perceived political pressures, they can hardly be seen as contributing to the strengthening of that condition. If private sector leaders look the other way when pollutants are dumped in the sea in violation of the law, they are threatening the conditions of rule of law and ecological understanding.

Leaders—public, educational, and private sector—all have to help watch out for the dangers posed by democracy itself. Near the end of Volume Two of *Democracy in America,* Tocqueville gives us a much-quoted (and much-ignored) sense of the subtle ways in which an "immense tutelary power," one "detailed, regular, far-seeing, and mild," will move:

> It covers its surface with a network of small, complicated, painstaking, uniform rules through which the most original minds and the most vigorous souls cannot clear a way to surpass the crowd; it does not break wills, but it softens them, bends them, and directs them: it rarely forces one to act, but it constantly opposes itself to one's acting; it does not destroy, it prevents things from being born; it does not tyrannize, it hinders, compromises, enervates, extinguishes, dazes, and finally reduces each nation to being nothing more than a herd of timid and industrious animals of which the government is the shepherd.[55]

Such cautions are not to suggest that democracy (or any other government) is per se bad. We do, of course, need some government, despite concerns about overreaching and despotism and an overreaching state. When everything is left to the private sector, elementary services can be difficult to come by. For example, David Landes notes that "in Ottoman Turkey, firefighting was in the hands of private companies, who came running when the alarm sounded. They competed with one another and negotiated price with house owners on the spot. As the negotiations proceeded, the fire burned higher and the stakes diminished. Or spread. Neighbors had an interest in contributing to the pot. 'Twixt meanness and greed, many a house fire turned into mass conflagration."[56] We need our government. But we have to be mindful of the dangers of finding ourselves too much in need.

Leadership and Human Nature

The conditions we have been talking about do not derive from themselves; rather, they are grounded in some sort of view of human nature. Spoken or unspoken, calculations of human nature ground any assessment of necessary political behavior. For example, in his discussion of the uses of ambition to counteract ambition and the usefulness of connecting self-interest with the interest of society, James Madison notes that "it may be a reflection on human nature, that such devices should be necessary to controul the abuses of government. But what is government itself but the greatest of all reflections on human nature? If men were angels, no government would be necessary. If angels were to govern men, neither external nor internal controuls on government would be necessary."[57]

Another reflection on human nature that has a direct bearing on these conditions is found in the monologue of Dostoevsky's Grand Inquisitor. As reported by his creator, Ivan Karamazov, the Grand Inquisitor faces down the Christ who has come back to

Inquisitorial Spain in the 1500s. The Grand Inquisitor has Christ arrested. In the middle of the night, the Inquisitor comes to Christ in the dungeon and berates Christ for offering people freedom. Do you not know, the Inquisitor asks, that people do not want freedom? You offered them freedom; we corrected your error. We let the people do what they please in inconsequential things, but overall, we know, as do they, that it would be better not to have too much freedom. We have assumed the burden of freedom, of choice, for them, and they are happy to be ruled by us with miracle, mystery, and authority. Such is the Grand Inquisitor's view of human nature.

We may not have a Grand Inquisitor in our time, but we do have those whose views are similar to his—people who would at least make the argument that freedom is not necessarily a good thing, and it is better to focus on security and order at the expense of freedom, if only for the public good. Singapore, with its great wealth, its great emphasis on order and punishment, and its curiously stultifying lack of political opposition, comes to mind.[58]

The extent to which one believes that justice is obtained by individual character or by societal institutions is another critical aspect of how one defines human nature. In his life of Dion, Plutarch suggests that the security of the state does not rest on "fear and force, a great fleet and a host of barbarian bodyguards, but rather out of the goodwill, the loyalty and the gratitude which are engendered by the exercise of virtue and justice."[59] But there is another view, one arguably put forth by Machiavelli. In "What Is Political Philosophy?" Leo Strauss makes clear the distinction in discussing how Machiavelli has been easily given "perfect respectability" in Western thought. Machiavelli, says Strauss, "can be presented as arguing as follows: you want justice? I am going to show you how you can get it. You will not get it by preaching, by hortatory speeches. You will get it only by making injustice utterly unprofitable. What you need is not so much formation of character and moral appeal, as the right kind of institutions, institutions with teeth in them. The shift from formation of character to trust in institutions is the characteristic corollary of the belief in the almost infinite malleability of man."[60]

One way or another, explicitly or implicitly, we guide our actions as leaders by some sort of view of human nature. The notions of management and supervision that were put under the rubric of Theory X some years back assumed that human beings were lazy and in need of considerable direct supervision if production were not to go to hell in a handbasket. A counter-set of notions, commonly put under the Theory Y rubric, assumed a contrary position: human beings were alert, capable, desirous of doing well and working hard; in fact, they would work even harder with less supervision.[61]

As Herbert Muller put it, "For all the dispute over the character of Cromwell and his works, we may at least agree that he meant it when he said, 'It is not what they want, but what is good for them—that is the question.' This is indeed the perennial question, forced two thousand years before Cromwell by Plato in his *Republic*, as later again by the Grand Inquisitor."[62]

When leaders undertake to lead, to persuade, to contribute to a more thoughtful public, what they are doing, either explicitly or implicitly, is working on the basis of some sort of calculation of human nature. That calculation, that basic view, cannot be prescribed here or by any other means. What we can suggest, though, is that if a leader wishes to understand himself or herself as part of understanding the larger sense of leadership in the political context, it is important to face head on one's own views of what, at base, human beings are and do. Moreover, the more you make known your basic views of human nature, the more others will understand the basis for your attempts at persuasion. Others may not agree with you, but your willingness to be explicit, and their understanding of what you are saying, will contribute to a more honest and open encounter.

Securing the Conditions for Democracy: The Role of Schools

To be an effective leader in a democracy, whether in the public sector, the schools, or the private sector, it is necessary to have a people who understand the conditions necessary for a democracy—a people who understand the demands, tensions, and contradictions of a democracy.[63] Leaders need to recognize the connection among leadership, a democratic civic society, and education of the people. If leadership is situated in the larger political regime and if we want a democracy, a free democratic society, and if a democracy depends on conditions being in place, and if those conditions have to be learned by people if they are to govern themselves wisely, then all leaders—not just public leaders or educational leaders, but all leaders, including private sector leaders—had best provide for and support good schools to teach people their moral and intellectual responsibilities for living and working in a democracy, to be a more thoughtful public. If we do not have good schools, then we will not have good citizens. Without good citizens to support a free, democratic society with knowledge, intelligence, and understanding, there will be little to sustain a society in which leaders can truly lead.

Leaders must insist on what Madison (and the other Founders) insisted on. There must be an enlightened citizenry armed with knowledge to protect themselves against tyranny. With such knowledge, Madison said, "a popular Government, without popular information, or the means of acquiring it, is but a Prologue to a Farce or a Tragedy; or, perhaps both."[64] If for no other reason than prudence and the desire to keep doing business as usual without massive government interference that necessarily comes from despotic and authoritarian regimes, leaders should recognize the need to support schools that in turn support the enculturation of the young into a political and social democracy.[65] This kind of enculturation will help develop, Ralph Lerner suggests, "the technical skills and moral lessons that might render the people safe and knowing guardians of their own liberty."[66]

What I am talking about here is not just the usual pious cant about schools that litters so much of the rhetoric of politicians and other leaders. I am talking about leaders' taking an active part in ensuring that schools are doing more than producing students who have high test scores. The creation of good schools as places for the enculturation of youth into a democracy does not require the total preoccupation of every leader. Leaders, even school leaders, have other responsibilities too. But attention to the schools is an important part of leadership, involving more than just that one-day visit to the classroom every year or so. Leaders need to support efforts to ensure that schools are effective in preparing the young for citizenship in a democracy. In a self-governing society, there must be, as Raymond Aron suggests, "a moral discipline established, as it were, in the individual conscience. The citizens must be subject, within themselves, to a discipline which is not imposed merely by the fear of punishment." Moreover, Aron says, "It is not enough to have the institutions of freedom: elections, parties, a parliament. Men must also have a certain taste for independence, a certain sense of resistance to power, for freedom to be authentic."[67] It is in large part in schools that citizens develop that taste and that resistance.

Schools have much to do with the creation and sustenance of a free, democratic society. Through schools, and thus through maintaining that society, leaders of all kinds will be assured of maintaining a political context that allows for the greatest amount of freedom, flexibility, and responsibility, allowing them best to pursue their own interests as well as the interests of the entire community.

5

Leadership, Reconciliation, and Reconstitution

It is a part of life that things fall apart. The First Pair were barely in the Garden for a minute or two before the temptation of knowledge proved too strong, and shortly after leaving Eden, one son was slain by the other. Since that distant time, much has changed, but with remarkable persistence things still fall apart. Our clichés and admonitions tell us as much. A stitch in time saves nine. There's no crying over spilled milk. Look before you leap. Our nursery rhymes suggest as much. Humpty Dumpty doesn't just sit there. He falls off, and there is nothing much to be done for him. Our dramas, too, reflect things going wrong (otherwise they would not be dramas). Some say that *Hamlet* would not be much of a play if Hamlet did his uncle in at the beginning of Act 1, Scene 1. But we would not have a play at all if Hamlet's father had not been killed, if peace reigned, if the economy remained stable, and if Hamlet acceded to the throne with the acclaim of all after his father died of natural causes at a ripe old age.

The notion of things falling apart extends across time and space. From a document of the Song dynasty of the tenth to thirteenth centuries, we find that "people of wisdom and understanding know that trouble cannot be escaped, so they are careful in the beginning to guard themselves against it. . . . After all, calamity and trouble, slander and disgrace, could not be avoided even by ancient sage-kings, much less by others."[1]

People in organizations are not immune to things falling apart. Things fall apart for us in the public sphere, in schools, and in the private sector. The question, then, is what role leaders have to play when things fall apart. What should they do? How should they respond? What we need to visit here is the particular notions of how things fall apart and how we traditionally respond when they do. And we need to explore what I trust will be effective and ethical ways of recovering, reconciliation, and reconstitution.

Things go wrong in lots of ways in the public sphere, schools, and the private sector. In the public sphere, one can be doing a reasonably good job as, say, the mayor of a large city, only to be faced with a huge and really quite unexpected blizzard and not enough snowplows. An irate public can show its lack of sympathy at the polls in the next election. In schools, a controversy over *Huckleberry Finn* or *Catcher in the Rye* erupts just two weeks before a crucial levy election; things finally get back to normal and the parents quit picketing the board meetings, but the levy proposal is defeated.

In the private sector, it is a truism that many things can go wrong. Despite solid research, new-product marketing is always a bit of a pig in a poke. Even well-established products can be threatened. New Coke replaced Old Coke for a time, until it was apparent just what a failure the new product was.[2] What we are able to do in many such instances, however, is try to repair the damage fairly directly. When news of the Tylenol tampering first hit, the manufacturer followed a pattern of full disclosure from the beginning and was able to recover quite quickly; its public relations response to something going wrong continues to be cited as exemplary.[3]

Things go wrong in planning large projects. The Sydney Opera House was finally completed ten years behind schedule at a cost of fifteen times the original estimate. The Concorde's cost increased tenfold over the original estimate.[4] The high-tech baggage system designed for the Denver International Airport never did work.

Things can really go wrong on a much larger scale. As depicted in such movies as *Dr. Strangelove* and *Failsafe*, nuclear war can happen quite by accident.

Indeed, many things can and do go wrong despite our good intentions. The New York Harbor cleanup is one of hundreds of examples of unintended consequences Edward Tenner discusses in *When Things Bite Back*. The water is cleaned up. Fish return. All is well. Or is it? The population of shipworms and gribbles had been suppressed by the petrochemical pollution; once that pollution was reduced, the shipworms and gribbles returned in full force, chewing up wooden piers in a matter of two years. The water is clean, but pier replacement in New York Harbor alone will costs hundreds of millions of dollars.[5]

Above all, things go wrong between people. Here we are not talking about technology, or big projects, or accidental nuclear war, but the smaller, more modest, but absolutely critical relationships between people. Relationships founder, sometimes for no apparent reason. Who knows what causes such things? A fictional social worker, dealing with two estranged sisters, gives us a summary of what happens to many people: "These family quarrels, I know what they are. Someone said something and the other one answered, and you stop talking to each other except on the coldest and most formal basis. And most of the time neither party can remember what started the coldness in the first place."[6]

Sometimes the falling apart can stem from different views of the political order. John Adams and Thomas Jefferson were close for a time, then fell apart during the conflict between the Federalists and the Republicans, culminating in the bitter election of 1800. For many years after, the two remained silent toward each other, finally reaching an accommodation (and giving us a wonderful series of letters) in late 1811.[7] We return to their reconciliation later in this chapter.

Sometimes the falling apart can be deliberate. Thomas Powers argues that life divides us into winners and losers, and "the winners in life do not forget their old friends; the old friends withdraw. . . . The greater his ambitions once were, the harder it is to accept his own ordinariness, and the more painful it is to see old friends. The 'drifting apart' to which old friends are supposed to be subject to is not, I would argue, a form of drifting at all. . . . It strikes me as a separation as deliberate, if not as formal, as a divorce." Many of us spend a good deal of time brooding about failure, Thomas says, and thus "when a friend embarks on certain projects with a high casualty rate—like writing a novel or running for public office—I know we are heading for a cool and distant period. I don't ask certain friends what they are working on now because I know how much they will suffer if they tell me, and certain friends don't ask such questions of me."[8]

Sometimes the falling apart can happen quickly. Marcel Mauss cites a Melanesian feast in which one chief invited another chief and his people. Dances were performed all night long. "By morning everyone was excited about the sleepless night of song and dance. On a remark made by [one chief] one of the [other chief's] men killed him; and the troop of men massacred and pillaged and ran off with the women of the village." This occurred even though the two chiefs "were more friends than rivals."[9] So fast can these things happen—in Melanesia, here, anywhere else—that it is a wonder that relationships survive. We ask, "What did I say?" and "What did I do?" when one moment we seem to have at least a modicum of a working relationship, if not friendship, and with a word, a look, the relationship is turned on its head.

It does not take much to set things off. In times of yore, the fairy who was not invited to the christening curses the new baby. In our time, faculty members sort out who was on the "A" list and who was on the "B" list to the dean's annual house party, and remember all too well that they were in the latter and did not like the insult. From such little things in a path-dependent way, we can end up making somewhat serious decisions about our organizations because of someone's having taken offense over a holiday party invitation.

What we find—not always and not everywhere but often enough and widespread enough—are such behaviors as lack of cooperation, resentful silence, grudges, cabals, plots, office politics, deliberate withholding of information (or provision of deliberately misleading information), lying, gossip, distortion, and mythmaking. Again, there are many organizations where such behaviors do not obtain, at least not on a regular basis, but there are many organizations in which people are behaving in ways similar to Cormac McCarthy's description of eating with the Tarahumara: "There was nothing to drink. No one spoke. The Indians were dark almost to blackness and their reticence and their silence bespoke a view of the world provision, contingent, deeply suspect. They had about them a wary absorption, as if they observed some hazardous truce. They seemed in a state of improvident and hopeless vigilance. Like men committed upon uncertain ice."[10]

How We Respond When Things Go Wrong

There are many ways in which we can respond when things fall apart between people and between other people and ourselves. Let us look at seven of these ways within the context of organizations, people in those organizations, and ourselves as leaders.

One way to respond is to do nothing—because we do not even *know* what is going on. People on the staff are divided into camps; some have retired to their caves, others are engaging in passive-aggressive behaviors, and some leaders proceed with no knowledge of the situation. Sometimes the lack of awareness stems from having too sharp a focus on other things. Bright light does make for deep shadows, and acuity in some areas is often accompanied by blindness in others. Some leaders might still believe in the old adage, "When ignorance is bliss, 'tis folly to be wise." If such leaders knew some of the things going wrong between people in their organizations to the detriment of morale, productivity, and profits, they would find little sense in the adage and would take steps to learn what was going on around them.

A second response is to try to ignore a bad situation. This is different from not doing something because we do not know what is going on. To ignore implies at least a little knowledge of the situation. But sometimes we elect to ignore because we do not want to deal overtly with the situation, or because we do not want to give the situation status (or further life) by acknowledging it. The advantage of this response is that it takes little energy or resources, at least in the short run. The disadvantages, however, can be considerable. For most of us, trying to ignore behavior that is in fact irritating or threatening or simply bothersome takes more energy than we might realize. We come to understand that we are probably not going to change that behavior by ignoring it (wishing for extinction while drumming our fingers and casting our eyes to heaven) and that when we do finally act, we wonder, irritated at ourselves, why we did not make a move earlier. Thus, when we do cease ignoring behavior and escalate to active opposition against it, we sometimes act more strongly (and usually less effectively) because of our irritation at the other person and at ourselves. We know that riot police will suffer taunts and bottles thrown at them, and will suffer for a goodly time, hoping the crowd will disperse. But when the tipping point is reached, and enough is enough, police efforts at "crowd control" can be excessive, with lots of pepper spray and baton wielding.

A third kind of response involves justifying and excusing the breakdowns between people. Sometimes the advantages of this response seem to be support from one camp or another. "I certainly can understand why you folks feel the purchasing department is treating you so shabbily" might make people feel you are on their side. And there is considerable support for the notion that an important part of leading is listening to others and assuring them that you understand their point of view. In the mid-1700s, Lord Chesterfield advised his son that "many a man would rather you heard his story than granted his request."[11] But unless you move beyond feeling people's pain and empathizing with them, sooner or later those same people will begin to wonder whose side you are on, given that you understand but do nothing to help them. In the end, justifying and excusing might be understandable responses, honest reactions to a bad situation. But these are enabling responses that by themselves will do little to change the situation.

A fourth response is to remove the people who appear to be causing difficulties. In *Orestes*, Euripides shows us a traditional way out of the never-ending cycle of revenge:

> Suppose a wife murders her husband.
> Her son then follows suit by killing her,
> and his son then must have his murder too
> and so on.
> Where, I want to know, can this chain
> of murder end? Can it ever end, in fact,
> since the last to kill is doomed to stand
> under permanent sentence of death by revenge?
> No, our ancestors handled these matters well
> by banning their murderers from public sight,
> forbidding them to meet or speak to anyone.
> But the point is this: they purged their guilt
> by banishment, not death. And by so doing,
> they stopped that endless vicious cycle
> of murder and revenge.[12]

In ancient Greece, banishment was one way out of the bind. In our own time, we are sometimes tempted to banish or fire those we see as troublemakers. As the saying goes, "He who is absent is always in the wrong." Sometimes we try to fire people who are in one camp or the other, thinking that it takes two camps to make a fight, and if one camp is gone or greatly weakened, there will be some peace and quiet.[13] Sometimes the firing can proceed without too much pain. For example, the president of an organization hired a bright young assistant. It became obvious to everyone that the bright young assistant wanted the president's job. Indeed, the assistant said as much to the president. The president fired his assistant. It was a relatively amicable firing; the two remained colleagues and political allies over the years. However, as most leaders have experienced, it is really quite difficult to fire people solely because they are not getting along with us or with someone else in our organization. Obviously one can fire someone for cause, say, for grand theft or criminal negligence. But it is very difficult to fire people because they are pouting, being resentful, casting a pall over things, making life miserable for others by their constant complaining or bickering or plotting.

A fifth response involves revenge, getting even, when we think we are threatened or wronged—a relatively serious form of office politics. One archetype here is found in Edgar Allen Poe's "The Cask of Amontillado," with Montresor deliberately setting out to take revenge on the man who has wronged him. As Montresor teaches us, "A wrong is unredressed when retribution overtakes its redresser. It is equally unredressed when the avenger fails to make himself felt as such to him who has done the wrong." One curious aspect of this classic tale is that we never know the nature of the transgression, the wrong. For all we know, it may just be in Montresor's mind.[14] Another archetype is Hamlet, who spends most of his time in the play trying to sort through the task given him by his dead father's ghost: "If thou didst ever thy dear father love . . . revenge his foul and most unnatural murder." It is a difficult task to unseat a standing, popular king, a task that keeps Hamlet occupied throughout the play. Some might argue that revenge will clear the air, and better to have clear air and the honest light of day than to have things fester. Some say that getting even is the best revenge; some even say that revenge is a dish best tasted cold. But surely this response has all sorts of limits. Francis Bacon saw revenge as "a kind of wild justice, which the more man's nature runs to, the more ought law to weed it out."[15]

In *Death and the Maiden*, Ariel Dorfman gives an example of the limits (and dangers) of revenge. Paulina takes revenge against the doctor she believes had tortured her, but it is not clear whether she even has the right man, let alone whether she has the right to violate the rule of law.[16]

A preoccupation with getting even or restoring honor (as with dueling, a kind of revenge or getting even) means that other tasks within the organization will not receive full attention. And when the work is not getting done and your superiors inquire as to the reasons, whatever honor that was served or whatever delights that were tasted by getting even will seem pitifully small.

A sixth response is to acknowledge the bad situation but keep the lid on through force, threats of force, or forced cheerfulness. An example often cited is Tito's policies in Yugoslavia, with some arguing that Tito kept the lid on ethnic tensions by refusing to let anyone acknowledge that anything was wrong. Although there is considerable argument over the impact of these policies, we can at the least argue that with his "Brotherhood and Unity" slogan, Tito was attempting to keep things quiet rather than solve underlying problems.[17] On a lesser level, we might note the university dean who responded to dissidence among the faculty by making everyone read and sign a statement of mission and objectives. Perhaps those who follow such papering-over strategies assume that if people are forced to behave in certain ways, after a time they will come to believe what they signed. Other kinds of papering over include singing company songs.

The seventh response is to run from the bad situation. In *The Segmented Society*, Robert Wiebe gives us a useful discussion of three fundamental conditions that would govern the development of American society. These conditions are worth discussing in some detail, given their broad and continuing influence. One condition was the sheer expanse of land, an expanse that "invited those people who had differences to solve their problems by separation instead of accommodation. Rather than adjust, they parted. . . . Where hostile Catholics and Protestants found themselves neighbors, as in Maryland, they fought only so long as it took their camps to disperse. . . . Differences were spread across space rather than managed within it." Wiebe points out that "inside the communities life concentrated increasingly upon distinctions among the like-minded, giving daily human relations a peculiar, prickly quality of nuance. . . . Rather than assisting diverse groups to function within a common sphere, they articulated those values everyone was expected to accept."[18]

Another condition was the freedom from military threats in America, which allowed freedom to go about one's affairs. "Major portions of Europe emerged from the era of the French Revolution with a new awareness of the nation as a social whole that bound even those who hated or despised each other to an ultimate accommodation. Because Americans escaped the traumas of war, they also escaped that sense. . . . If people hated or despised each other, they could simply live apart. An ultimate accommodation was not merely unnecessary; it was unnatural."[19]

A third condition was economic abundance: "Only in a land of plenty could people have sustained their faith that interdependent groups living side by side need not break the barriers between them and scramble over an apportionment of the nation's wealth. While abundance had been facilitating separation since the seventeenth century, in the twentieth it rationalized an entire system, a compact society of interrelated but insular parts."[20]

Given these conditions that Wiebe identified, we can derive a reasonably clear picture as to why we did not, early on in the history of the United States, feel it all that necessary to deal with problems between individuals and between groups. And given that at least two of these conditions no longer exist in the United States, it is reasonably clear that we must begin to deal directly with conflict, strife, and different ways of viewing things when they go wrong. The alternative is to watch things go terribly wrong, as viewed from our vantage point in gated communities or as heard over our short-wave radio in the Idaho wilderness.

These several responses might in some instances be reasonable and effective. Sometimes it is more effective all around to fire someone or ignore a problem. But surely we need to find better ways of dealing with the problems of things going wrong between people. Most of these responses are to ignore or run from or run over serious breakdowns between people—breakdowns that affect morale, productivity, and happiness. These are ethical matters, then: we have choices in how to respond when things fall apart. They are ecological matters in the sense that small things over time (sometimes a very short period of time) can lead to major and intended consequences. What leaders need to attend to, beyond ignoring, running from, or running over, is reconciliation and reconstitution. Leaders need to try to make things whole, to say what others cannot or will not say, to pick up the pieces and begin anew—if not with the old whole, then a new, reconstituted whole. To reconcile and reconstitute is to take on a great deal, requiring much ingenuity and patience on the part of the leader. As a first step in finding these better ways to respond, we must develop a better understanding of what motivates people and what needs to happen to people so they can move on. What moves people? What accounts for things falling apart between people?

Motivations Leading to Things Falling Apart

A consideration of motivations can reasonably begin with Samuel Johnson's observation: "We are all prompted by the same motives, all deceived by the same fallacies, all animated by hope, obstructed by danger, entangled by desire and seduced by pleasure."[21] It is, to be sure, a complex picture, this being human. "Power is exercised by human beings, who are, of course, extraordinarily complex," Mancur Olson suggests. "As I see it, human beings rarely act out of unmixed motives. There is not only self-interest but also a benevolent element—and even a malevolent streak—in human nature."[22] That malevolent streak is what Huck Finn cannot help but notice as he watches his former tormentors, the "king" and the "duke," get tarred and feathered. The two "didn't look like nothing in the world that was human." Huck goes on to say, "Well, it made me sick to see it and I was sorry for them poor pitiful rascals, it seemed like I couldn't ever feel any hardness against them any more in the world. It was a dreadful thing to see. Human beings *can* be awful cruel to one another."[23]

People are moved for all sorts of reasons (and sometimes for no reason at all). In what follows, I am not considering all of the range of motives. I am considering those motives that tend to relate to things going wrong. I am suggesting that we consider what most people would see as the less positive and more negative aspects of human beings. We have to think about irrationality, suspicion, capriciousness, self-destruction, ambition, greed, emotions, craziness, jealousy, envy, avarice, competition, uncertainty, resentment. And we have to think about how easily things can slide. A little word here and there, a little misunderstanding, and off we go.

People get angry easily, and they do not always listen carefully, leading to further misunderstanding. Aristotle suggests that "anger seems to listen to argument to some extent, but to mishear it, as do hasty servants who run out before they have heard the whole of what one says, and then muddle the order, or as dogs bark if there is but a knock at the door, before looking to see if it is friend; so anger by reason of the warm and hastiness of its nature, though it hears, does not hear an order, and springs to take revenge. For argument or imagination informs us that we have been insulted or slighted, and anger, reasoning as it were that anything like this must be fought against, boils up straightaway."[24]

People get angry very quickly. They can brood, too, as Joseph Conrad observes in *The End of the Tether:* "He brooded profoundly, after the manner of crafty and unintelligent men."[25] We can observe brooding among the crafty and intelligent, both men and women, after a bad staff meeting, when they think another camp has won, when they think their ideas have not been attended to, when they think they have not been allowed to talk. Resentment can set in. The nameless clerk in Dostoevsky's *Notes from Underground* gives us a powerful sense of how people can build up resentments. As one critic notes, "What the reformers of the Enlightenment, dreaming of a perfect organization of society, had overlooked, Dostoevski saw all too plainly with the novelist's eye: Namely that as modern society becomes more organized and hence more bureaucratized it piles up at its joints petty figures like that of the Underground Man, who beneath their nondescript surface are monsters of resentment."[26]

Many people resent having to comply, especially with someone else's ideas: "The inclination to demand compliance with one's ideas is a more extreme and aggressive trait than the brutal demand to somebody to relinquish some of his possessions."[27]

Ambition is another motivation in human beings, and as with other motivations, it is complex and problematic, reaching in the directions of both good and evil. Cecil Rhodes claimed, and we can probably take him at face value here, "I would annex the planets if I could. I think of that often. It makes me sad to see them so clear and yet so far."[28] And perhaps we are not far from the Faust of Part II, with our ambitious seeker after power and control sending Mephistopheles out to remove the old couple from their cottage and seize their property in order to build a great tower, the better to oversee his domains.

Ambition sometimes stems from a feeling of inadequacy, especially when we compare ourselves to others. Francis Bacon gives us a sense of this kind of ambition: "Men of noble birth are noted to be envious towards new men when they rise. For the distance is altered; and it is like a deceit of the eye, that when others come on they think themselves go back. . . . Near kinsfolks, and fellows in office, and those that have been bred together, are more apt to envy their equals when they are raised. For it doth upbraid unto them their own fortunes, and pointeth at them, and cometh oftener into their own remembrance, and incurreth likewise more into the note of others; and envy ever redoubleth from speech and fame."[29]

Sometimes the stress that contributes to things falling apart comes not from ambition for ourselves but from our ambitions for others. The transference of ambition—the implied sense that although we have failed, others whom we have ambitions for will be able to do well for themselves and make up for what we could not do—can be a considerable burden. In "Sentenced to Nature," a description of a survival training–wilderness therapy program for wayward teenagers, we are told of a parent who says to a program counselor, "I can't have it on my kid's record that he was here. He's going to be president of the United States."[30]

Sometimes ambition is coupled with pride, leading to anger, as Thomas Hobbes reminds us in *Leviathan:* "Pride, subjecteth a man to Anger, the excesse whereof is the madness called *rage*, and *fury*. And thus it comes to passe that excessive desire of Revenge, when it becomes habituall, hurteth the organs, and becomes Rage: That excessive love, with jealousie, becomes also Rage: Excessive opinion of a mans own selfe, for divine inspiration, for wisdome, learning, forme, and the like, becomes Distraction and Giddinesse: the same, joyned with Envy, Rage: Vehement opinion of the truth of any thing, contradicted by others, Rage."[31]

In "Letters from a Federal Farmer," John Dickinson warns that "we cannot act with too much caution in our disputes. Anger produces anger; and differences, that might have been accommodated by kind and respectful behavior, may, by imprudence, be enlarged to an incurable rage. In quarrels between countries, as well as in those between individuals, when they have risen to a certain height, the first cause of dissension is no longer remembered, the minds of the parties being wholly engaged in recollecting and resenting the mutual expressions of their dislike."[32]

Abraham Lincoln, echoing Dickinson (and in some sense Thucydides' description of the revolution at Corcyra), tells what can happen when things fall apart: "Deception breeds and thrives.

Confidence dies, and universal suspicion reigns. Each man feels an impulse to kill his neighbor, lest he be first killed by him. Revenge and retaliation follow. And all this, as before said, may be among honest men only. But this is not all. Every foul bird comes abroad, and every dirty reptile rises up. These add crime to confusion."[33]

Once things go wrong, they can stay wrong a long time, with people not necessarily knowing what caused the rift or the conflict in the first place. Ambition, anger, and grudges in turn can lead to feuds. In *The Adventures of Huckleberry Finn*, Mark Twain spends considerable time describing an ongoing feud between the Granger-fords and the Shepherdsons. Reminding us of Euripides and Orestes, young Buck Grangerford says he wanted to kill a Shepherdson man. Huck asks,

> "What did he do to you?"
>   "Him? He never done nothing to me."
>   "Well, then, what did you want to kill him for?"
>   "Why nothing—only it's account of the feud."

Buck explains to Huck what a feud is:

> "A man has a quarrel with another man, and kills him; then that other man's brother kills *him*; then the other brothers on both sides, goes for one another, then the *cousins* chip in—and by-the-by everybody's killed off, and there ain't no more feud. But it's kind of slow, and takes a long time."

Huck asks, "What was the trouble about, Buck?—land?"

> "I reckon maybe—I don't know."
>   "Well, who done the shooting—was it a Grangerford or a Shepherdson?"
>   "Laws, how do *I* know? It was so long ago."

"Don't anybody know?"

"Oh yes, pa knows, I reckon, and some of the other old folks; but they don't know, now, what the row was about in the first place."[34]

Finally, the motivations for behavior sometimes seem to come from nowhere, from just plain irrationality or cussedness. In *The March of Folly*, Barbara Tuchman speaks of folly of governments as counterproductive policies that were seen as counterproductive at the time, with other realistic options available, but not chosen.[35] We can see in others (and ourselves, should we wish to look carefully) every now and then a tendency toward self-destruction— the pursuit of objectives that are clearly not in our best interests. Moreover, we sometimes seem to behave with absolutely no purpose of any kind.

We tend to find the irrationality or lack of purpose more bothersome than what we see as reprehensible but purposeful behavior. In Alfred Hitchcock's movie *The Birds*, we see birds attacking human beings for no apparent reason. Perhaps that is what makes this movie so bothersome. We would prefer to have a reason. We would feel better if we were told that the birds are attacking because of some ecological disaster (as in science-fiction movies from the 1950s: the giant ants or spiders or sea monsters are products of nuclear weapons tests). We seek purpose in trying to understand political assassinations. We want to have a reason and will invent elaborate conspiracy theories that appear to explain a slaying because we cannot bear purposelessness or random acts of violence.

The motivations for behavior outlined here may well be seen as negative and unattractive. Are there no positive motivations? Is there nothing attractive about human beings? Of course, there are many positive, attractive motivations. People are often warm-hearted, trusting, willing to help each other out, go the extra mile without recompense; they take pride in their work and in their loyalty to the organization and their colleagues. When such motivations are in play and things are going well, the main problem leaders have is to sustain the circumstances that make for good relations and productive and happy employees. (To so sustain is a challenge in itself, with the difficulties entailed when things do go wrong.) My purpose here is not to deny positive and attractive motivations but to focus on motivations that contribute to things falling apart in order that we might better understand how to recover and reconstitute.

Approaches to Reconciliation and Reconstitution

Given the depth of feelings (and the variety of motivations) when wrongs are done or perceived to be done, it is clear that to fulfill responsibilities for reconciliation and reconstitution is no simple task. It is not at all clear how we might take on this task and fulfill our responsibilities as individuals or leaders in organizations. Where might we turn to develop an understanding of appropriate ways to reconcile and reconstitute or, even, whether in all circumstances we should have reconciliation and reconstitution in our sights? Let us turn first to what we might term large-scale reconciliation efforts to see what we might glean from the experience and observations of others, then turn to reconciliation on the no-less-important scale of individual to individual.

The examples of large-scale attempts at reconciliation are legion. The aftermath of the Civil War in the United States. Slavery and its aftermath, with continuing effects of even now. The aftermath of internment of Japanese Americans during World War II. Germany after World War II and the Holocaust. The aftermath of the Khmer Rouge in Cambodia. The reconciliation process in South Africa. The aftermath of the repression in Chile. Much has been written about these (and many more) attempts at reconciliation. From some of these accounts we can draw lessons that may help us in less terrifying but still trying and difficult circumstances.

Trying to understand the difficulties of reconciliation in Chile, Ariel Dorfman comments on his play *Death and the Maiden*:

> As I began to write I found the characters trying to figure out the questions that so many Chileans were asking themselves privately but that hardly anyone seemed interested in posing in public. How can those who tortured and those who were tortured co-exist in the same land? How to heal a country that has been traumatised by repression if the fear to speak out is still omnipresent everywhere? And how do you reach the truth if lying has become a habit? How do we keep the past alive without becoming its prisoner? How do we forget it without risking its repetition in the future? Is it legitimate to sacrifice the truth to ensure peace? And what are the consequences of suppressing that past and the truth it is whispering or howling to us? Are people free to search for justice and equality if the threat of a military intervention haunts them? And given these circumstances, can violence be avoided? And how guilty are we all of what happened to those who suffered most? And perhaps the greatest dilemma of them all: how to confront these issues without destroying the national consensus which creates democratic stability?[36]

Timothy Garton Ash raises similar questions in his review of books dealing with national transitions from difficult pasts: "Whether to remember and treat the past at all, in any of the diverse available ways, or simply to try to forget it and look to the future; when to address it, if it is to be addressed; who should do it; and finally, how?"[37]

The reconciliation efforts in South Africa, most notably the work of the Truth and Reconciliation Commission, have been discussed at great length by many observers, including the chairman of the commission, Archbishop Desmond Tutu.[38] Tutu's arguments for full reconciliation and full social harmony in turn have been scrutinized by others. David Crocker contrasts Tutu's concept of reconciliation as social harmony with two other possibilities: "nonlethal coexistence" and "democratic reciprocity." In nonlethal coexistence, reconciliation occurs when former enemies no longer kill each other or routinely violate each other's basic rights. This thin sense of reconciliation, attained when cease-fires, peace accords, and negotiated settlements begin to take hold, can be a momentous achievement. Crocker argues that nonlethal coexistence is easier to realize than Tutu's ideal that requires friendliness and forgiveness. With democratic reciprocity, Crocker argues, "former enemies or former perpetrators, victims, and bystanders are reconciled insofar as they respect each other as fellow citizens," and all parties will have a voice in deliberations over the past, present, and future of their country. Democratic reciprocity is difficult, but still easier than an ideal of mutual compassion and the *requirement* of forgiveness. In fact, Crocker suggests, "some would argue . . . that there are unforgivable crimes or point out that a government should not insist on or even encourage forgiveness, since forgiveness is a matter for *victims* to decide."

Crocker's critique of Tutu's approach toward the ideal of social harmony concludes that Tutu "pays insufficient attention to individual freedom, including the freedom to withhold forgiveness. In making social harmony the supreme good, Tutu unfortunately subordinates—without argument—other important values, such as truth, compensation, democracy, and individual accountability."[39]

Crocker offers eight objectives of transitional justice that societies trying to deal with human rights violations should work toward: (1) disclosure of facts (that is, "reasonably complete truth with respect to the past"), (2) a public platform for victims to tell their stories, (3) meting out of sanctions to those responsible, (4) compliance with the rule of law and due process, (5) public deliberation and a fair hearing, without "requiring unanimity or consensus,"

(6) recommendations for removal of causes leading to past abuses, (7) reconciliation, at least in the sense that while former enemies "may continue to disagree and even be adversaries, they live together nonviolently and as fellow citizens," and (8) "promotion of good long term changes such as further democratization and just economic development."[40]

Of these eight, the notion of public deliberation is of particular importance to Crocker. A society in transition should "engage in a society-wide discursive process in which the merits of various proposals for the ends and means of transitional justice are publicly debated and judged. . . . Likewise, democratic bodies, accountable to the public, should decide how and why the society should reckon with past evil. Moreover, the results of these choices—such as legal decisions or investigatory reports—should be publicly available. . . . In a society aspiring to be liberal and democratic, public deliberation expresses the commitment to respect one's fellow citizens, to engage in give-and-take, and to forge compromises with which all can live nonviolently."[41]

Another approach to large-scale reconciliation efforts is found in the foreword to John Lederbach's *Building Peace*. The argument here is for "the creation of societies currently riven by division and violence of 'sustainable peace,' by which the author means a good deal more than the already difficult tasks of brokering a cease-fire, negotiating a peace settlement, or implementing a multifaceted peace accord. Sustainable peace requires that long-time antagonists not merely lay down their arms but that they achieve profound reconciliation that will endure because it is sustained by a society-wide network of relationships and mechanisms that promote justice and address the root causes of enmity before they can regenerate destabilizing tensions."[42]

Lederbach argues that "peacebuilding must be rooted in and responsive to the experiential and subjective realities shaping people's perspectives and needs." He suggests a framework for reconciliation that includes the notion of relationship: "Reconciliation is not pursued by seeking innovative ways to disengage or minimize the conflict groups' affiliations, but instead is built on mechanisms that engage the sides of a conflict with each other as humans-in-relationship."

Moreover, there must be an encounter: "People need opportunity and space to express to and with one another the trauma of loss and their grief at that loss, and the anger that accompanies the pain and the memory of injustices experienced. Acknowledgment is decisive in the reconciliation dynamic. It is one thing to *know*; it is yet a very different social phenomenon to *acknowledge*. Acknowledgement through hearing one another's stories validates experience and feelings and represents the first step toward restoration of the person and the relationship."

Lederach concludes that reconciliation must engage: "*Truth* is the longing for acknowledgment of wrong and the validation of painful loss and experiences, but it is coupled with *Mercy*, which articulates the need for acceptance, letting go, and a new beginning. *Justice* represents the search for individual and group rights, for social restructuring, and for restitution, but it is linked with *Peace*, which underscores the need for interdependence, well-being, and security."[43]

One lesson seems clear: not recognizing the past, not coming to terms with the truth, is costly and debilitating for all parties. One recurring example of the costs is the refusal of the Japanese government to acknowledge the claims brought by "comfort women," Korean women who were sexually abused in brothels run by the Japanese Army in the 1930s and 1940s. An observer notes that the courts might legally be right in tossing out the lawsuits brought by many of the aggrieved, "but surely there is no statute of limitations on saying sorry for such egregious wrongs done within living memory. . . . A statement of contrition is all the more deserved since politicians can still be found who vow, contrary to evidence, . . . that the women and girls—some only ten years old— locked up and abused in the army's brothels were prostitutes who volunteered their services. . . . The events Japan is now being asked to apologise for took place more than a half century ago. Isn't it time to move on? Indeed it is. But facing up to the past is the way to avoid having to live in it. . . . [Japan would] stand immeasurably taller in Asia, if it said sorry, directly and unambiguously, to the women whose lives its army so deliberately shattered."[44] Japan might stand taller, when viewed from afar, but it seems that a combination of pride and a reluctance to deal with the resentment others have when a leader apologizes are factors that militate against Japan's taking such a step.

It is a complex and delicate matter, this notion of apology, forgiveness, and knowing when to move on. In *Wild Justice*, Susan Jacoby argues that "'forgive and forget' is . . . not only an impossible admonition but an undesirable one; it implies a lack of respect for the profound sense of moral equilibrium impelling us to demand that people pay for the harm they have done to others. The entire modern argument over the relationship between revenge and justice turns on this question of the equilibrium between memory and hope."[45]

Michael Ignatieff, in *The Warrior's Honor*, sounds a similar theme:

> Leaders give their societies permission to say the unsayable, to think the unthinkable, to rise to gestures of reconciliation that people, individually, cannot imagine. In the Balkans, not a single leader had the courage to exorcise his nation's ruling fantasies.
>
> The chief moral obstacle in the path of reconciliation is the desire for revenge. Now, revenge is commonly regarded as a low and unworthy emotion, and because it is regarded as such, its deep moral hold on people is rarely understood. But revenge—morally considered—is a desire to keep faith with the dead, to honor their memory by taking up their cause where they left off.

> Revenge keeps faith between generations; the violence
> it engenders is a ritual form of respect for the commu-
> nity's dead—therein lies its legitimacy.[46]

Ignatieff goes on to say that

> reconciliation can stop the cycle of vengeance only if it
> can equal vengeance as a form of respect for the dead.
> What each side, in the aftermath of a civil war, essen-
> tially demands is that "the other side" face up to the
> deaths it caused. To deny the reality of these deaths is to
> treat them as a dream, as a nightmare. Without an apol-
> ogy, without recognition of what happened, the past can-
> not return to its place as the past. . . . Reconciliation has
> no chance against vengeance unless it respects the emo-
> tions that sustain vengeance, unless it can replace the
> respect entailed in vengeance with rituals in which com-
> munities once at war learn to mourn their dead
> together.[47]

We have to acknowledge the past while not getting bogged
down in it. And we have to do more than acknowledge the past. As
Ignatieff suggests, we have to find ways to allow people to honor the
past while transcending it. In all respects, this is a most difficult but
necessary task. Francis Bacon tells us, "That which is past is gone,
and irrevocable; and wise men have enough to do with things present and to come; therefore they do but trifle with themselves, that
labour in past matters."[48] On the other hand, as a character in
Requiem for a Nun puts it, "The past is never dead. It's not even
past."[49] But we know that we do have to deal with the past. And
how do we do this when the prevailing sentiments from school
boards, boards of regents, corporate boards of directors, and a vot-
ing public tend to echo Bacon's approach, with tremendous pressures to focus on next quarter's earnings, next semester's school test
scores, and next year's need for a tax increase?

From the large-scale reconciliation attempts and the lessons we might draw, we turn now to examples of reconciliation between individuals. The scale is perhaps smaller, but the lessons to be gleaned are by no means less important.

Sometimes forgiveness is expressed indirectly, with statements put on the table for others to look at and accept. Near the conclusion of *The Iliad*, Homer tells us of a partial reconciliation that is offered by King Priam. Priam's son, Hector, has been slain by Achilles. Priam goes to the camp of Achilles to ask for his son's body. Achilles and Priam weep together, then Achilles offers food. As they are eating, Priam says that this is the first food he has eaten since the death of his son. Another instance of partial or indirect reconciliation is found in our own time at the end of *The Outlaw Josie Wales*, Clint Eastwood's epic movie about revenge in the post–Civil War era. One of the bounty hunters finally catches up with Wales, now living under a different name. Instead of arresting Wales, however, the long-time pursuer tells Wales and his friends that he is heading south, and maybe he'll catch up with his man there. And then what? asks Wales. Looking Wales directly in the eyes, the pursuer says, "I think I'd try to tell him the war is over." "I reckon so," says Josie.

The reconciliation of Jefferson and John Adams, brought about by Benjamin Rush, is a wonderful example of reconciliation. Even before the election of 1800, Adams and Jefferson had political differences that strained friendship. Following the election, the two had little contact. Abigail Adams sent a note of condolence to Jefferson in 1804 following the death of his daughter. In response, Jefferson made opening moves toward reconciliation, but Abigail was unsympathetic. There was silence for eight years. Benjamin Rush, friend of both Adams and Jefferson, worked for more than two years at reconciliation. His tactics of persuasion included a convenient dream in which he reads a history of the United States detailing the renewal of friendship between the two ex-presidents, the resumption of their correspondence, and, startlingly enough, the notion that the two "gentlemen sunk into the grave nearly at the same time." Adams dismissed that October 1809 dream as history, although he allowed that "it may be Prophecy." (We might say both history and prophecy, given that Adams and Jefferson both died on July 4, 1826.)

Rush kept at his reconciliation attempts and found another opening when in 1811 a friend of Jefferson visited Adams. To this mutual friend, Adams said, "I always loved Jefferson, and still love him." When word got back to Monticello, Jefferson wrote to Rush, "That is enough for me," indicating he was willing to open up correspondence with Adams. Rush forwarded Jefferson's comments to Adams, diplomatically leaving out Jefferson's observation that "from this fusion of mutual affection, Mrs. Adams is of course separated. It will only be necessary that I never name her." On January 1, 1812, the celebrated correspondence opened with a letter from Adams to Jefferson. Even then, there were possibilities for misunderstandings. Adams tells Jefferson he is sending along by separate post "two Pieces of Homespun." Jefferson took this as a reference to clothing, and in his first letter back to Adams he talked at length about clothing manufacture in Virginia. Adams had in fact sent under separate cover the two volumes of John Quincy Adams's *Lectures on Rhetoric and Oratory*. Later in the correspondence, they avoided controversial subjects for the most part but remained friends.[50] The reconciliation ultimately involved John and Abigail Adams, Thomas Jefferson, and their good and faithful friend, Benjamin Rush, with Rush operating with patience, imagination, and more than a bit of subterfuge. The reconciliation process was difficult, and it took time.

Another example of a difficult and complex reconciliation over time is given to us by Eric Lomax, a Scottish military officer who volunteered for the Corps of Signals during World War II. In *The Railway Man*, Lomax relates how he became a prisoner of war after the fall of Singapore in 1942 and ended up working on the infamous Burma-Siam Railway. Caught with a makeshift radio, Lomax was tortured and beaten. He survived, but two others who had been caught with him did not. Years later, Lomax was still suffering the trauma of his experience and was nursing a painful and debilitating hatred of his tormentors. One day his wife brought his attention to a newspaper account of a guilt-ridden Japanese man who had spent years trying to atone for his part in the interrogation of a British soldier, one British soldier in particular. He felt that at long last, after many visits to the Kanburi cemetery, he was forgiven; his guilt, he thought, had "vanished." From the accompanying photos, Lomax recognized the man as one of his tormentors, the interpreter during the many fearsome interrogations. His first reaction was strong and understandable: "I wanted to damage him for his part in ruining my life."

His wife, Patti Lomax, reacted strongly too. She wrote to Nagase Takashi, the interpreter, wanting to know how Nagase could feel pardoned when her husband had not yet forgiven him. Nagase replied, saying he wanted to meet with Lomax and that her letter had made him think again about his guilt: "The dagger of your letter thrust me into my heart to the bottom." Patti found Nagase's letter "extraordinarily beautiful." Eric had a similar reaction: "Anger drained away. In its place came a welling of compassion for both Nagase and me, coupled with a deep sense of sadness and regret. In that moment I lost whatever hard armour I had wrapped around me."

Over a period of some months, Lomax and Nagase exchanged a series of letters. They finally met, at the bridge at the River Kwai, near Kanchanaburi, Thailand. Lomax recounts his changed feelings: "I could no longer see the point of punishing Nagase by a refusal to reach out and forgive him. What mattered was our relations in the here and now, his obvious regret for what he had done and our mutual need to give our encounter some meaning beyond that of the emptiness of cruelty." More was needed, however. "Assuming that our meeting, in itself, constitutes forgiveness, or that the passage of time had made it irrelevant, seemed

too easy; once someone raises forgiveness to such a pitch of importance you become judicial. I felt I had to respond to Nagase's sense
of the binding or loosening force of my decision." In the end,
Lomax finds "the right moment to say the words to [Nagase] with
the formality that the situation seemed to demand," meets again
with Nagase, and gives him a letter in which "I told him that
while I could not forget what happened in Kanburi in 1943, I
assured him of my total forgiveness. [Nagase] was overcome with
emotion again, and we spent some time in his room talking quietly and without haste."[51]

There is much to be learned in this powerful and moving story.
Forgiveness comes not easily; it is a struggle, a struggle that in the
end is worthwhile. The form of forgiveness matters a great deal, and
the form must be meaningful to both parties struggling to find common ground. Forgiveness here is not unilateral; Nagase at one point
says that his guilt has vanished, but Patti reminds Nagase that her
husband has not forgiven him. (Here the position is similar to what
Richard Crocker suggests earlier in this chapter: "Forgiveness is a
matter for *victims* to decide.") Nagase needs *formal* forgiveness, and
Lomax meets this need with the letter exchange at the second
meeting. As with the Adams-Jefferson reconciliation, Lomax and
Nagase need more than themselves (although they are obviously
central and most critical). Their wives are involved, as are the staff
counselors at the Medical Foundation for the Care of Victims of
Torture. Moreover, they need time, and they need to work things
out in their own way.

These few examples of individual reconciliation are powerful in
themselves. And they remind us of the limits of governmental
action. Gesine Schwan suggests that given that "real renewal has
to come from a voluntary, inner act, we have to recognize that in
the last resort we cannot rely exclusively on enforceable, institu-
tional strategies, but have to fall back on free discussion and persuasion. We must also recognize that *in the moral field, the private
sphere is vitally important.*"[52]

Reconciliation and Reconstitution:
What We Need to Do

For leaders, for all of us, to fulfill responsibilities for reconciliation and reconstitution will take an altering of deep structures and not just superficial change. Sustainable reconciliation and reconstitution are, to use terms from bodywork and therapeutic massage, a kind of structural realignment or Rolfing that has long-term effects. Rolfing deals with realignment of the fascia and stretching of tendons and ligaments that have shortened and become contorted over time—far different from a superficial body massage that leaves one feeling good for an hour or two but does nothing to alter the deep structure significantly. Given the focus on deep structure and given the lessons we can derive from even a brief consideration of large-scale reconciliation and individual reconciliation, what should leaders realistically try to focus on?

Following are six suggestions for action, provided with the caveat of contingency. As suggested by those observing and analyzing large-scale reconciliation, much depends on circumstance, on the context; what might be appropriate in one situation might be highly inappropriate in another. Nonetheless, some general suggestions can be offered.

First, we need to see the world large, not small. In *The Confessions of Felix Krull,* Thomas Mann speculates on which way to see the world: "I would ask myself: which is better, to see the world small or to see it big? The significance of the question was this: great men, I thought, field marshals, statesmen, empire-builders, and other leaders who rise through violence above the masses of mankind must be so constituted as to see the world small, like a chessboard, or they would never possess the ruthless cold bloodedness to deal so boldly and cavalierly with the weal and woe of the individual."[53]

Seeing the world large (that is, in great detail) can be a virtue, as suggested in the ancient Taoist classic, *Huainanzi:* "No one stumbles over a mountain, but people do trip over anthills."[54] We can get so caught up in the mission and objectives and strategic futures plans and the "big ideas" that we sometimes overlook the little things that turn out to be not so little.

Second, we cannot lie to ourselves and others. In *The Brothers Karamazov*, Father Zosima gives this advice to Fyodor Karamazov:

> Above all, do not lie to yourself. A man who lies to himself and listens to his own lie comes to a point where he does not discern any truth either in himself or anywhere around him, and thus falls into disrespect towards himself and others. Nor respecting anyone, he ceases to love, and having no love, he gives himself up to passions and coarse pleasures, in order to occupy and amuse himself, and in his vices reaches complete bestiality, and it all comes from lying continually to others and to himself. A man who lies to himself is often the first to take offense. It sometimes feels very good to take offense, doesn't it? And surely he knows that no one has offended him, and that he himself has invented the offense and told lies just for the beauty of it, that he has exaggerated for the sake of effect, that he has picked up on a word and made a mountain out of a pea—he knows all of that, and still he is the first to take offense, he likes feeling offended, it gives him great pleasure, and thus he reaches the point of real hostility.[55]

We need to see ourselves clear, not lie to ourselves. And we must not lie to others; we must see them clear as well. Again, we are faced with a most difficult task here. It is hard enough to see ourselves clear. It is even harder to understand others with honesty and respect. Michael Ignatieff notes "how self-deceiving we are about our needs. By definition a person must know that he desires something. It is quite possible, on the other hand, to be in need of something and not know that one is. Just as we often desire what we do not need, so we often need what we do not consciously desire." Ignatieff extends this: "If we often deceive ourselves about what we need, we are likely to be deceived about what strangers need. There are few presumptions in human relations more dangerous than the idea that one knows what another human being needs better than they do themselves."[56] (Ignatieff is close to Pascal with these sentiments. Pascal argued that "we are nothing but lies, duplicity, contradiction, and we hide and disguise ourselves from ourselves.")[57] We can listen, too, to the counsel of the *Huainanzi:* "If the leader cannot minutely discern people's psychological conditions, and the feeling of those below is not communicated above, then above and below oppose each other and matters are disordered. This is how leadership goes to ruin."[58]

Third, we can insist on seeking the truth about what has happened, and we can develop a process that will engage all parties in honest and public deliberation. (Here, of course, "public" does not necessarily mean the general public. A college departmental faculty can engage in public deliberation, if it so chooses, as opposed to furtive and unsatisfactory meetings in the parking lot.)

Fourth, we can make the time and resource commitments necessary to an authentic process of reconciliation and reconstitution. If the time and resources are not available, then the process will be seen as merely pro forma (and insulting, and a waste of people's time, and, moreover, an egregious attempt at covering up problems). You might decide that reconciliation and reconstitution are not desirable ends, and you have good grounds for the decision. But at the very least, it is important that you make the decision in a conscious way, alert to the ethical and political consequences.

Fifth, we can recognize the relationship between reconciliation and reconstitution and a free, democratic society. Again, we need to consider Richard Crocker's argument that "in a society aspiring to be liberal and democratic, public deliberation expresses the commitment to respect one's fellow citizens, to engage in give-and-take, and to forge compromises with which all can live nonviolently." Gesine Schwan suggests that "the unwillingness to acknowledge guilt, the silencing of guilt, damages the political culture of a democracy because it hinders the realization of a vivid and motivating consensus on the common values of a polity and because it damages the psyches of perpetrators as well as their children, so that it becomes difficult for them to develop the strength of personal identity necessary for good citizenship."[59]

Sixth, we need to recognize that the elements of reconciliation, such as trust, openness, give-and-take, honesty, public deliberation, and critical inquiry into the past, are likely to be found in a free and open regime and not in a regime that is authoritarian and not free. Virtually all of the characteristics of a free, democratic regime outlined in Chapter Four are directly linked to authentic processes of reconciliation and reconstitution. Notions of justice, trust, social capital, exchange, free and open inquiry, knowledge of rights, and so forth have a direct relationship. It is hardly likely that a dictatorship engaged in flagrant human rights violations is at the same time going to proceed with an open and authentic investigation into its own actions.

It may seem obvious that public leaders, and even school leaders, must have some understanding of the need for a free, democratic society if they are to do their work. Private sector leaders will also have a strong vested interest in helping to sustain a free, democratic society if they are to engage in authentic efforts at reconciliation and reconstitution, because, following the arguments in Chapter Four, it is difficult for the private sector to operate in ways far divergent from the larger political and social regime. It will be easier for the private sector to proceed with openness and honesty in examining the past and seeking the causes for things falling apart when the larger society places a high value on honesty, openness, and critical inquiry. We might also note here that leaders seeking to deal on a sub rosa basis in hiding the truth will have a much easier time of it in an authoritarian regime with tight control over the media, and a much more difficult time of it in a free society.

Two caveats are in order here. First is a reminder. The focus on reconciliation and reconstitution is not intended to suggest some sort of bland "forgive and forget." We are not talking about being a doormat or letting bygones be bygones.

Second, some of the traditional responses we have when things fall apart might well be the best solution. For example, firing someone may well be the best response to a difficult situation all around, assuming you have the legal and moral authority for firing. Or, to take another example, ignoring (or pretending to ignore) a bad situation might be the most effective strategy. Thus, although I have stressed that getting at the truth is a necessary part of reconciliation, there may be times when getting at the truth is not going to be productive. Let's say that a faculty member in a department is causing much trouble for colleagues with self-centered and irrational behavior. To set things right with a process of reconciliation would involve much time and much diversion of resources to the task. If the chances are that the faculty member will be at the institution for years to come, with no option of transfer or firing available to the department head, then one strategy might well be to try to work things out, which would involve getting at the truth in a public way. But if the department head knows that the faculty member is likely to transfer to another institution, then a prudent strategy might be to ignore the situation, wait things out, and have a good-bye party.

Conclusion

How to deal with things falling apart is not easy, particularly when what is falling apart are relationships between people, with bad feelings, hurt feelings—the whole range of emotions examined in this chapter. Reconciliation and reconstitution are difficult matters.

They need to be part of our larger efforts as leaders. As leaders, we have to create organizational environments that are productive and ethical. Moreover, we have to sustain those environments. Sustaining is not simply trying to preserve in amber our creation, because there are too many changes in the larger environment to allow such unchanged preservation. Moreover, given that things do go wrong, we have to engage in a process of reconciliation and reconstitution not to recover the past but to make a better future.

It is not easy. But our understanding of what needs to be done when things go wrong is vital. Many years ago, I used to watch Julia Child perform her cooking magic once a week on television. It was always interesting to watch her techniques and approaches leading to a perfect soufflé or a glorious hollandaise sauce. But what made her program really valuable was its unrehearsed nature. Things would go wrong from time to time. The hollandaise would separate. Far from being a disaster for Julia Child, it was an opportunity for her to show us how to recover, to reconstitute, by mixing a small bit of sauce in with a bit of lemon juice, then a little more, and the sauce was back together. Given that in my enthusiasm and hurry, I was more likely than not to beat more butter into the hollandaise than could be absorbed, my knowing how to reconstitute the sauce was of much greater importance to me than knowing how to make it perfectly.

To know how to lead when things are going well is useful knowledge. Perhaps more useful is the knowledge of what to do, and of what one ought to do, when things fall apart.

6

Reflections and Directions

W e are near the end of our tour, back to where we started, and although we do not now know it precisely for the first time, I trust we have a somewhat different sense of what it means to be a leader in a democracy. It is time to savor that sense—time to pause, take stock, look over the terrain, and reflect on what we have seen and determine where we might want to go.

Returning to the Major Elements of Leadership

One guide who can help us take stock is Sophocles, speaking to us across some twenty-five centuries through his subtle and compelling play *Philoctetes*. Let us turn to a brief summary of the action in this play and then consider the lessons we can draw from it, and from there, the lessons we can draw from our explorations in the previous five chapters.

Ten years have passed since Philoctetes, a Greek warrior, has been bitten by a snake on board the ship carrying him and his fellow warriors to Troy. He suffers a horrific and painful wound. His constant moans disturb the other warriors. At long last, they set Philoctetes ashore on a deserted island. Here for ten years he is by himself, able to survive only by hunting with his bow, a magic bow given him by Heracles. The bow is indeed magic; whatever Philoctetes shoots at is brought down. When the play proper opens, we are shown Odysseus, the crafty trickster warrior, and his young companion Neoptolemus, son of Achilles. They are making their way back to the deserted island. We are given to understand (as ancient Greek audiences would of course already have known) that Odysseus has been told to get Heracles' bow from Philoctetes. Odysseus has been told by the oracle that without the bow, Troy will not be conquered. The difficulty is that Philoctetes, having been abandoned ten years earlier by Odysseus and his mates, will be unwilling to give up his bow, Odysseus tells young Neoptolemus. He will not be open to persuasion. On the other hand, they will not be able to get the bow by force, given the bow's magic qualities. What to do?

Odysseus comes up with a plan. He tells Neoptolemus to land on the island and tell Philoctetes that he is fed up with the war and wants to go back to Greece. Philoctetes will become distracted, and Neoptolemus can steal "the arms no man has conquered." Neoptolemus is not inclined toward trickery, as Odysseus knows, so the crafty old persuader spins his argument thus:

> I know, young man, it is not your natural bent
> to say such things nor to contrive such mischief.
> But the prize of victory is pleasant to win.
> Bear up: another time we shall prove honest.
> For one brief shameless portion of a day
> give me yourself, and then for all the rest
> you may be called most scrupulous of men.

They argue back and forth. "Do you not find it vile yourself, this lying?" asks Neoptolemus. "Not if the lying brings our rescue with it." "How can a man not blush to say such things?" As a good utilitarian, Odysseus replies, "When one does something for gain, one need not blush." Finally, Neoptolemus gives in. He will go ashore, trick Philoctetes, get the bow, and they will be off.

At first, the trickery goes according to plan. Philoctetes is overjoyed to find that Neoptolemus is headed back to Greece, and even more overjoyed when Neoptolemus agrees to take Philoctetes with him. An attack of his sickness comes on Philoctetes. He must sleep, he says, while Neoptolemus guards his bow. And while he sleeps, Neoptolemus takes the bow, although he is beginning to understand what Odysseus does not (or chooses not to): "I see we have hunted in vain, vainly have captured our quarry the bow, if we sail without him. His is the crown of victory, him the God said we must bring."

When Philoctetes awakes, Neoptolemus tries to persuade him to sail to Troy to fight with the other warriors. Philoctetes pleads with Neoptolemus to give him back his bow. Odysseus appears on the scene, telling Neoptolemus to come with him. They leave Philoctetes behind. He curses them, saying he will never go to Troy. A bit later, Odysseus and Neoptolemus come back. Neoptolemus says, "I go to undo the wrong I have done." He has returned to give the bow back to Philoctetes: "To my shame, unjustly, I obtained it." Odysseus threatens to take the bow by force, but Neoptolemus has the bow and thus the upper hand. Odysseus skulks away. Philoctetes appears. Neoptolemus repents his trickery and gives the bow back. Odysseus reappears. Philoctetes tries to kill him but is restrained by Neoptolemus. Odysseus again skulks away. Neoptolemus tries without success to persuade Philoctetes to come to Troy. Philoctetes is adamant. Only when Heracles appears on the scene, the deus ex machina, telling Philoctetes that he must indeed go to Troy to fight, does Philoctetes give his assent.

With this basic summary of the action in mind, we can begin to see the major elements of leadership outlined in the previous five chapters. Let us examine these elements one by one.[1]

Persuasion

There are three ways to do business here, according to Odysseus: force, persuasion, or trickery. Force will not work. Persuasion is unlikely to work. So Odysseus uses trickery. But as we can see, trickery does not work either. First Neoptolemus, then Neoptolemus and Philoctetes together, work around Odysseus. The only choice for

Odysseus is to withdraw, grumbling that he is going to tell on them to his companions (sounding rather like a vanquished bully). Odysseus is no longer a player. The only approach that has a possibility of resulting in a solution that will work to everyone's satisfaction is persuasion. Even here, persuasion does not work. But it is the only strategy that might work; the other two are bound to fail.

For ourselves, we can learn from the errors that Odysseus made. If open, honest persuasion is not going to work for us, then perhaps we need to step back and reassess the situation. Are we really in such a hurry that force or trickery must be relied on? I once asked a leader why she had not gone ahead with a given action when she probably could have made the necessary moves without too much of a risk. "Because I didn't have the community with me, and if they weren't ready to move, I couldn't move until they were ready," was the reply.

Once we do decide to try to persuade rather than use force or trickery, we need to listen to the opposition as we develop our plans. Odysseus could have listened to the concerns that Neoptolemus expressed; instead, he overrode them. When we marshal our forces of persuasion, we often go barreling ahead, convinced of our rightness. Sun Tzu (and many others) warned against underestimating the enemy. In similar manner, we should not underestimate those whom we might try to persuade; we should not underestimate their knowledge, their interest, their awareness; nor should we underestimate their sensitivity to tone and nuance. Thus, in developing our arguments of persuasion, we should share drafts of what we have in mind with people to get their cognitive and affective reactions to what we are proposing. They should be free to express themselves without fear, they should have no need to toady, and at least some should have relatively little background knowledge or technical understanding of our arguments and the particular situation in question. This sharing and listening actively to reactions takes time, but it takes a lot more time to pick up the pieces after sending out a memo that people misinterpreted or were offended by.

Information Seeking

Odysseus has it from the oracle that he must get the bow in order
to prosecute the war against Troy successfully. But Odysseus has
become too focused here; he misinterprets the oracle's directive.
The bow is only a part of what is needed. What is needed is for
Philoctetes to rejoin the community. Without Philoctetes, the bow
by itself is nothing. Neoptolemus comes to recognize this. He is the
younger, the less experienced, but in this respect he is wiser than
the old trickster Odysseus. (Here Odysseus is close to Croesus, king
of Lydia. In 546 B.C.E., Croesus camped by the river Halys in Asia
Minor, ready to make war against the Medes and Persians camped
on the other side of the water. Before invading, he consulted with
the oracle of Delphi as to his chances. The oracle's message said that
if he crossed the river, he would destroy a great empire. Reassured,
Croesus went to war—but the empire he destroyed was his own.)

What we learn here is an old lesson, an obvious one even, but
given the number of times we ignore it, the lesson is worth revisit-
ing, as we did in Chapter Two. We should not bias our information
seeking. We should not mold information to fit our preconceived
opinions of what should be. We should constantly be aware of how
easy it is to seek and process information selectively. And we should
always be aware of the larger—and always subtle—context in which
to seek information and in which to put the information we obtain.

Ethics and Ecology of Rhetoric

Go ahead and lie, counsels Odysseus. "For one brief shameless portion of the day," be unethical and tricky, and from then on, you can
be ethical and virtuous. But there is an ethics of rhetoric, and an
ecology of rhetoric, and once Neoptolemus goes down the path of
the shameless rhetoric, there is no turning back.

For us, we are sometimes tempted to lie or, if not to lie outright,
to use specious arguments and (with Thucydides) "fair phrases to
arrive at guilty ends." As we discussed in Chapter Three, there are

times when we use diplomatic prudence because we do not want to hurt someone. Sometimes a euphemism is appropriate because the plain term in the circumstance is just too brutal and hurtful for others (and ourselves) to face. Perhaps rhetorical guile or arguments that appeal to the less edifying aspects of human existence will "work" for a while, but in the long run, they will not. How we choose to persuade will catch up with us one way or another.

Reconciliation and Reconstitution

The critical thing is to get Philoctetes back into the community, as Neoptolemus now understands. It is not enough to get the bow. But trust has been violated. Although Philoctetes has his bow back and an apology from Neoptolemus, his violation is too great. Only the intervention of Heracles—a miracle, if you will—allows the play to end as it needs to, with Philoctetes agreeing at long last to rejoin the warriors. Had Heracles not so intervened, we would be at a standstill. No amount of persuasion, however heartfully felt, would move Philoctetes once the distrust engendered by trickery is upon him. A sobering thought.

One of our urgent tasks as leaders is to accomplish reconciliation and reconstitution. This is always a difficult task, and often a task we cannot accomplish. It will be much harder to reconcile and reconstitute, however, if we have first tried trickery (and trickery comes in all kinds of guises) because we did not want to take the time and resources authentically to bring people back together again. We will find many people like Philoctetes—people who are alienated and resentful (often with good reason) and immune to our pleading. The main difference between the situations before us and the situation Philoctetes was in is that we have no Heracles to come to our aid to make everything whole. There is little magic in the real world.

Despite the lack of magic, there are occasions when reconciliation is effected, and all come together in a new and honorable way, through patience, negotiation, and listening. We have talked about

some of these occasions in Chapter Five. Another example can be found in the third part of the *Oresteia*. Aeschylus tells of the Furies: they feel rejected and dishonored, because they are to be displaced by the new religion of rationalism. The Furies threaten to "let loose on the land the vindictive poison dripping deadly out of my heart upon the ground." Athene tries to persuade them; the Furies refuse to budge. Finally, Athene tells them they will have an honored place, with full privileges. The Furies begin to shift their position, as indicated by their response: "Lady Athene, what is this place you say is mine?"[2] Athene tells them it will be a place "free of all grief and pain. Take it for yours." The Furies then move to a negotiating mode: "If I do take it, shall I have some definite powers?" Athena assures the Furies that they will have an honored role in human affairs.

Again, reconciliation and reconstitution are the order of the day here. As with Philoctetes, the Furies have to be reintegrated into the community to become part of the regular rhythms of life. No clever trickery, no amount of clever "bottom-line" analysis will brook the conclusion that without reconciliation and reconstitution, things simply won't work in the long run.[3]

What we learn from *Philoctetes* and the *Oresteia* and other ancient sources in the West is confirmed by similarly ancient and wise sources in the East. The ancient texts are replete with variations on the observation that "everything exists in relation to other things."[4] If we forsake our relationships, we stand a good chance of vanishing, or at least being greatly diminished.[5]

What we learn, too, is that leaders must have high expectations of those they would lead, especially if they wish to reconcile and reconstitute. To bring people out of their caves and back into the community, leaders have to expect more, expect the best. I am convinced that it would have been possible, just possible, for Neoptolemus to persuade Philoctetes to join the warriors against Troy had he dealt straight with Philoctetes to begin with. One critical element of the persuasion would have had to include high expectations on the part of Neoptolemus—expectations that an honorable and heartfelt appeal to Philoctetes would have been recognized for what it was and acted on as such.

Two other examples of high expectations of this kind come to mind here, one from Dostoevsky and the other from Winston Churchill. A critical point in *The Brothers Karamazov* comes when Aloysha is trying to deal with the death of his mentor, Father Zosima. He and a companion visit Grushenka, who has been planning to seduce the young Aloysha, the innocent from the monastery. She sits on his lap, then finds out about the death of Father Zosima. She immediately gets off his lap, appalled and apologetic. Aloysha thanks Grushenka, telling her she is his sister, a good person. Grushenka is astonished: Aloysha has appealed to her higher sense of herself, her better nature. And she responds in kind.[6]

Early on during World War II, Churchill asked, "What kind of a people do they think we are?" He made the British people think better of themselves at a time when there were a goodly number of folks who might have thought it convenient to settle with Hitler. As C. P. Snow notes, "Each of us knew people who were not to be trusted if the test came . . . people who . . . would have taught us the meaning of the word collaborator." But, Snow says, those who might have been tempted "couldn't live it out, in the face of Churchill and the forces he spoke for. Of course they weren't going to settle. Churchill knew that. And, of course, they did not."[7]

The Cultural-Political Context of Leadership

Odysseus, Neoptolemus, and Philoctetes cannot act outside of their culture or political regime. They must act within it, dealing with the consequences of their actions within a cultural-political context of shame, obligation, truth, trust, repentance. The great questions remain. How are we supposed to behave? What happens if we do not behave as we should? We are not ancient Greece, but we are in our own culture, and we have to behave within it, not outside it. To some extent, culture shapes behavior. But at the same time we can to some extent shape our culture, encouraging, say, an open, democratic, civic culture rather than a despotic one.

One of the ways we can shape this culture is through our schools. As we saw in Chapter Four, schools need to play a critical role in the enculturation of the young into a political and social democracy. Leaders—public, school, private sector—need to insist that schools take this role seriously and not simply be suppliers of a labor force, however important productivity in a society might be. What those schools need to do is emphasize what Odysseus misses. As James Boyd White puts it, what Odysseus misses

> is the reality of the social world, and its power. His cast of mind, which itemizes the world into a chain of desiderata and mechanisms, is incapable of understanding the reality and force of shared understandings and confidences. This error appears today in the common idea that our "wealth" is material—the bringing of resources under individual control for purposes of exchange or consumption—while in fact our most important wealth is social and cultural: confidence in the reliability and good sense and generosity of our neighbors; trust in the reciprocal practices by which community is established; pleasure in finding, and making, shared meanings, and in elaborating them collectively.[8]

Schools need to be based on and need to act on the knowledge that our most important wealth is social and cultural. This is an important role for schools. But we should not in our enthusiasm for the schools' role in enculturation and social capital overlook an equally important role: the provision of good education as an end in itself.[9]

The creation and sustenance of a healthy political and cultural context are critical. The efforts at reconciliation that we have talked about in this book suggest as much. Achilles and King Priam reconcile for a time, for a moment. But they have no real way out of the warrior culture they are in, no way to secure long-term reconciliation. Josie Wales reaches, with his adversary, a recognition of the futility of war, but in the end, Josie is seen riding off to places unknown, not back to the small community of which he had become a part. Eric Lomax and Nagase Takashi reconcile, but they live thousands of miles apart, not in the same community. John and Abigail Adams do reconcile with Jefferson; part of the same culture, they have a somewhat easier time of it. For us, however, we are here with each other—neighbors, coworkers, members of Tocqueville's voluntary associations. We have no other place to go when disputes arise between us. We surely cannot, as early colonists could, allow our quarrels to last only as long as it takes to break camp.

Final Reflections

I close this chapter, and thus this book, with reflections on change strategies, on the particular situation of the newly arrived leader, and on the goodness of Blake's "Minute Particulars" and real people.

The Need to Reconsider Change Strategies

My comments here will be brief. There is a vast literature on change and the change process; little of it can be essayed in this short space. My concern, rather, is to suggest that we reconsider what we say we do (as well as what we actually do) in the name of change, given the elements of leadership offered in this book, especially the elements focusing on reconciliation and reconstitution and their complications.

We know there is a reluctance to change even when things are not going well. Herodotus confirms our own experience: "If one were to offer men to choose out of all the customs of the world such as seemed to them the best, they would examine the whole number, and end by preferring their own; so convinced are they that their own usages far surpass those of all others."[10]

We know, too, that the effecting of change is a difficult matter at best. Once the change process gets under way, expectations are increased. Eric Hoffer reminds us that "our frustration is greater when we have much and want more than when we have nothing and want some. We are less dissatisfied when we lack many things than when we seem to lack but one thing."[11]

When people do not do what we want them to do, when they do not automatically follow along with what we propose, we say "they are afraid of change." And we bring in all sorts of consultants, change masters, and other experts we think will "help" our people understand that although change is threatening, change is a good thing. This strategy is but a transference, however; it is a way of avoiding the fundamental question as to whether the proposition for change is actually good. We avoid that fundamental question by saying, usually in patronizing ways, that people are threatened by change.

One response to these ways of talking about change by those who feel like Dostoevsky's "insulted and injured" is that they become even more cautious, crafty; they hide their feelings, like Satan does in *Paradise Lost:*

> Each perturbation smooth'd with outward calm,
> Artificer of fraud; and was the first
> That practis'd falsehood under saintly show,
> Deep malice to conceale, couch't with revenge.[12]

Far from being an open process leading to open information seeking, to rhetoric grounded on something other than expedience, and to reconciliation and reconstitution, these kinds of change strategies are often seen as inauthentic, leaving people unhappy and alienated.[13]

We should also note that there are quite legitimate reasons to act in opposition to an organization's proposed plans, even plans, say, for a process of reconciliation and reconstitution. Sometimes what is being proposed is really quite silly or counterproductive or even dangerous. Some people can see such things, and their opposition is real, principled, and worthy of attention and consideration. "Conflict resolution" or reconciliation is not what is needed in such circumstances. What is needed is clear thinking and a willingness to listen to unpopular opinions that are contrary to preconceived or received wisdom.

If we want to behave in better ways as leaders trying to persuade, to create more thoughtful publics, and to reconcile and reconstitute, we need to adopt change strategies that are congruent with these better ways.

The Particular Situation of the Newly Arrived Leader

It is difficult enough for comfortably established leaders to undertake the tasks suggested in this book. For newly arrived leaders, the challenges are even greater. It is not only that they are new leaders. Any leader coming into an organization will face difficulties in negotiating unknown terrain. But given what I choose to call the culture of administrative succession, the newly arrived leader will be in a particularly difficult position, especially with regard to the elements of leadership we have been exploring in this book. Let us look first at the culture of succession and then at the implications for leadership.

Most leaders move on. Rarely now does a leader stay in the same organization for an entire career. The years of long, comfortable tenure are long gone.[14] I recall looking at a long row of photographs of all those who had served as dean of the college of a certain university. The photographs were in chronological order, beginning with the first dean in the 1870s. There were relatively few photographs needed to encompass the period of the 1870s to the 1960s; twenty-year appointments were not unusual then. But by the mid-1960s, things began to change. There were three times as many photographs covering the twenty years. Acting dean was followed by acting dean, followed by a dean holding the post for a year or two, then an acting dean, another dean, and so forth. The comfortable years were no more.

What we must deal with as leaders ourselves, and in our relationships with other leaders, is not just the mobility, the turnover, the appearance of new people on the scene at an apparently increasing rate. What we must deal with is the culture of administrative succession.

The Culture of Administrative Succession

We know that organizational change takes a long time, and we know that we want *our* changes, carefully effected with much effort, to last a long time. At the same time, there is a lot of mobility, a lot of administrative turnover. Leaders leave; other leaders succeed them. The process of succession, part of a larger culture, has its own expectations, rituals, and rules—its own culture.

We are familiar with some aspects of this culture of succession. Territory is marked. A new office is chosen, as is new furniture (with sharp-eyed observers whispering about the cost of the classic Eames chair or the rosewood desk). Sometimes the "old" offices are occupied by the new leader, but they are painted anew, the furniture is rearranged, the carpets are replaced. Sometimes people are replaced, too, or rehired by the new leader. An inaugural speech is a familiar part of the culture, with the troops gathered together to hear the reassurances that all will be well, even better than in the past (as good as the past may have been). These are relatively benign aspects of the culture of succession, aspects we accept as part of the ritual of the new leader. But another aspect of the culture of succession poses difficulties.

If the culture of succession were characterized by a genuine desire to respect the past and if administrators were to be rewarded for maintaining and modestly improving what exists, there would not be as much of a problem as there is. But that is not the character of this culture. Rather, the culture of succession involves ambition, a focus on power and control, and pressures from hiring groups (such as boards of regents) to get a move on. All of these interact in particular ways to dump the past in favor of something new.

There is considerable ambition. Sometimes that ambition is reasonable (why would you want to be a leader unless you had some things in mind you would like to see done?), but sometimes that ambition moves to another, potentially more dangerous, level. In *Paradise Lost*, Satan says, "In my choice to reign is worthy ambition, though in Hell: Better to reign in Hell than serve in Heaven." Here we are in the realm of Cecil Rhodes, with his desire to annex the planets, in the realm of Herostratus who in 356 B.C.E. burns the Temple of Diana at Ephesus just to get fame. Abraham Lincoln was well aware of this kind of ambition and its dangers. In his insightful and disturbing speech, "The Perpetuation of Our Political Institutions," Lincoln warns against the highly ambitious man, the Caesar who needs fame and recognition, the kind of man who will, if he cannot get fame by building things up, will try to get fame by tearing things down. For this kind of ambitious man, whatever was done in the past will be ignored or replaced, Lincoln says. "Towering genius disdains a beaten path."[15] Perhaps Pascal was onto something in his observation that "the sole cause of man's unhappiness is that he does not know how to stay quietly in his room."[16]

Given the culture of succession, changes in leadership make for unsettling times. Given that culture and the highly likely ambitions of the new leader, there is a lot of worry, a lot of calculation on the part of those who have to say good-bye to the old leader while at the same time greeting the new boss. Commenting on the death of Augustus and the ascension of a successor, Tacitus said that people "must show neither satisfaction at the death of one emperor, nor gloom at the accession of another, so their features were carefully arranged in a blend of tears and smiles, mourning and flattery."[17] One has to appear to be loyal to the old order, but not so loyal that one might be seen as longing for the now-distant past, a laggard and potential opponent unwilling to get with the new program. On the other hand, if you jettison your loyalty to the past too quickly, the new leader might well wonder whether your new professions of loyalty will prove equally superficial and fleeting.

There are modest practical matters to deal with. Will my department remain influential? Will I be able to continue doing what I like to do? Will I be able to keep my office and my other perks? Will I finally be able to get a new computer, given what I think is the new leader's emphasis on technology? There are practical matters of time-consuming education of the newly arrived leader, trying to make sure the leader has at least a modicum of understanding of the worth of what you and your colleagues do.

Beyond these modest practical matters, however, lurks the threat of major change. In his *Essay on Man*, Alexander Pope tells us that "whatever is, is right." For the incoming leader, the motto often seems to be, "Whatever was, was wrong." As Alexander Hamilton comments in *The Federalist* No. 72, "To reverse and undo what has been done by a predecessor, is very often considered by a successor, as the best proof he can give of his own capacity."[18] And so the long-range plans and strategies carefully put into place during the previous administration, the little battles to bring people to think through and develop some sort of intelligent response—all of these run the risk of being cast aside in the name of the new, improved product. For those who have been in the organization for even a few years, the playing out of the culture of succession takes on a sense of Hegel's notion of history repeating itself, first as tragedy and then as farce. There are those who have heard it all before—the brave new vision statements, the mantras and the exhortations, the veiled threats—and for these people, the responses can range from just waiting it out (this person, too, will be leaving for more lucrative stock options or a chance to be an even bigger change agent somewhere else), to passive-aggressive behavior, to ignoring the new leader, to trying to do the best they can.

This unedifying picture of the newly arrived leader must be balanced by a consideration of other kinds of situations and circumstances. There are many organizations in need of a good overhaul—organizations in which complacency and laziness have displaced initiative and productivity, and a newly arrived leader is quite well within bounds to move for major change. My concern, however, is with situations less extreme—situations in which things are going along reasonably well. These sorts of situations are more problematic and pose more dilemmas than do the situations in which everyone agrees major overhaul is needed.

Implications for Newly Arrived Leaders

Given the culture of administrative succession, it is clear that the newly arrived leader will have some particular difficulties in dealing with the elements of leadership outlined in this book.

Newly arrived leaders, as with all other leaders, must be able to persuade others. Persuasion is particularly problematic for the new leader, especially for the leader who comes in with preconceived grand designs and with grand and sometimes fatuous statements. For example, Czar Alexander I says to the downtrodden and defeated, "I have come as a conqueror who seeks no other honour than the happiness of the vanquished."[19] It is difficult to see how people could have believed Alexander, and it is equally difficult to see how people might believe any newly arrived leader who claims that all is well, happiness of the workers is paramount, and there will be no major reorganization.

There is considerable pressure to ignore the past, and pressure to rush ahead with little awareness of how the troops are going to react. We know that any speech situation encompasses the speaker, the audience, and the speech situation. How well can the newly arrived leader calculate the effect of the speech on the audience? How can the newly arrived leader possibly understand the speech context?

Information seeking is particularly problematic. Part of the culture of succession focuses on speed. Everybody has to be a quick study. The newly arrived leader either has to gather information very rapidly or has to move ahead with a series of decisions bereft of possibly relevant information. As we noted in Chapter Two, seeking information is always a costly business. It is an activity that demands considerable reflection and strategy if the leader wants to avoid unwanted exchange relationships and political problems. To rush into information seeking increases the chances of problems and will often result in obtaining information that is wrong, biased, or otherwise calculated to make someone else look good or the new leader look bad. (Not everyone is going to be happy about the accession to the throne. Some will give partial information, just enough to provide an appearance of helpfulness, but in fact in the spirit of what Banquo tells Macbeth about the dangers of witches: "And oftentimes, to win us to our harm, the Instruments of Darkness tell us Truths; win us with honest trifles, to betray's us deepest consequence."[20] The newly arrived leader is for many an unwanted but necessary stranger, representing for some a threat, and for others an opportunity. In either case, the newly arrived leader is in a difficult position in seeking information, susceptible to all sorts of mischief.)

The alternative is to make big decisions, propose and direct new programs, hire and fire, all with relatively little information seeking. This alternative has the advantage of making the newly arrived leader appear to be moving things along at an astonishing and gratifying pace. But the disadvantages are legion. In addition to perhaps making errors because information was not sought, the newly arrived leader will be in a position to be attacked. After the first big fiasco, some of the onlookers at the crash site, veterans of the organization, will be heard to murmur, "I tried to say something, but B.R. just didn't seem to want to take the time to listen."

For some, being the new leader means a bit of a grace period, when one learns what's what, listens to people, seeks information, and gets settled in. This grace period usually does not last long. It is difficult to understand the context in which to place information and to sort out the subtly important from the unimportant. It is difficult, too, to sort people, when they are looking like the innocent flower but being the serpent under it (like Lady Macbeth). Part of the successful seeking of information is gaining the trust of others. Being in a hurry, the new leader might decide to be agreeable and amiable and welcoming. However, even this strategy might back-fire, as suggested in the *Tao Te Ching:* "If you agree too easily, you'll be little trusted."[21]

Efforts at reconciliation and reconstitution will be problematic for the newly arrived leader. In some instances, the leader has been hired specifically to deal with things that have gone wrong between people. The opportunities for making positive moves are apparently there, as is support from those who hired the leader in the first place. The new leader might want to deal with discord, but this can be hard when whoever hired the leader wants to get on with things, wants to solve what has gone wrong as quickly as possible so as to look to the future. As we noted in Chapter Five, reconciliation and reconstitution take time—time to determine how much of the past needs to be sorted out honestly and how much needs to be over-looked. From the perspective of those who hired the leader, the nec-essary time and effort might well look like a leisurely excursion into the past, and that is the last thing they want the new leader to indulge in.

One advantage of the new leader in bringing about reconcilia-tion and reconstitution is that simply by being new, the leader can sometimes inadvertently be the stimulus to bring warring factions together, at least on the surface. It is possible to move from a tem-porary truce, from the notion of "the enemy of my enemy is my friend," to the beginnings of real reconciliation and reconstitution.

The culture of succession is difficult to surmount. At best, what the newly arrived leader can try to do is adopt pro forma behaviors that appear to follow the rules of the culture, making obvious but in fact insignificant changes such as painting the office, getting a new rug, instituting new office procedures. These superficial changes can cover up what actually is a much slower pace, one that allows for much more cautious information seeking and decision making.

Minute Particulars and Real People

Even as we come to the end of the tour, back to where we started, my attempts at generalizing observations are brought up short by William Blake. In "Jerusalem," Blake tells us that "he who would do good to another, must do it in Minute Particulars. General Good is the plea of the scoundrel, the hypocrite & flatterer: for Art & Science cannot exist but in minutely organized Particulars and not in generalizing Demonstrations of the Rational Power."[22] Indeed.

In the end, if what we are to do as leaders is to make sense ethically and ecologically, we must stay low, stay down to earth. "The realities of life are most truly seen in everyday actions and things."[23] Dostoevsky warned of "giants" acting from what they thought were "principles" in order to aid humanity, while "neglecting the simplest and most obvious moral obligations. It was incumbent upon [such people] . . . to live up to their own pretensions, and to turn their abstract love of humanity into a concrete act directed toward a flesh-and-blood individual."[24]

And when we direct our acts toward real flesh-and-blood individuals, we need to pay close attention to what those individuals have to say. Thomas Hobbes observed that "to Value a man at a high rate, is to *Honour* him; at a low rate, is to *Dishonour* him. But high, and low, in this case, is to be understood by comparison to the rate that each man setteth on himselfe."[25] Close to Hobbes is English novelist Anthony Powell: "The General, speaking one felt with authority, always insisted that, if you bring off adequate preservation of your personal myth, nothing much else in life matters. *It is not what happens to people that is significant, but what they think happens to them.*"[26]

In the end, I am left with a real person, one depicted by Basho:

> A child of a poor family
> Stopped grinding rice
> To look at the moon.[27]

Notes

Foreword

1. Harlan Cleveland, *The Knowledge Executive: Leadership in an Information Society* (New York: Truman Talley Books, 1985).

2. John W. Gardner, *On Leadership* (New York: Free Press, 1990).

3. Christopher Hodgkinson, *The Philosophy of Leadership* (New York: St. Martin's Press, 1983), p. 10.

Chapter One

1. Euripides, *Hecuba*, 815, in David Grene and Richmond Lattimore (eds.), *The Complete Greek Tragedies*, trans. William Arrowsmith (Chicago: University of Chicago Press, 1958).

2. Thucydides, *Peloponnesian War*, trans. Richard Crawley (New York: Modern Library, 1951), 2:60.

3. Thucydides, *Peloponnesian War*, 1:138. In his commentary on Thucydides, Gomme notes that "Thucydides here says nothing of either the will or the ability to carry out a decision in practice; he ignores that astonishing power and energy which enabled Themistokles to impose his will on his colleagues at Salamis as well as his skill as a tactician. He is not in any way attempting a full-length portrait or a complete summary of Themistokles' character, still less of his own idea of the perfect statesman." A. W. Gomme, *A Historical Commentary on Thucydides* (Oxford: Oxford University Press, 1959), 1:443–444.

4. Thucydides, *Peloponnesian War,* 8:68.

5. Polybius, *Histories,* Book IV, 8.1, trans. W. R. Paton (Cambridge, Mass.: Harvard University Press, 1956).

6. Plutarch, "The Comparison of Demosthenes and Cicero," in *The Lives of the Noble Grecians and Romans,* trans. John Dryden (New York: Modern Library, n.d.), p. 1071.

7. Cicero, *De Oratore,* III, 59, trans. H. Rackam (Cambridge, Mass.: Harvard University Press, 1942).

8. Edward Gibbon, *The Decline and Fall of the Roman Empire* (New York: Penguin Books, 1994), 1:861–862.

9. Lord Chesterfield to his son, Dec. 12, O.S. 1749, in Bonamy Dobrée (ed.), *The Letters of Philip Dormer Stanhope, 4th Earl of Chesterfield* (New York: Viking Penguin, 1932), 4:1460.

10. Winston Churchill, *A History of the English Speaking Peoples,* vol. 3, *The Age of Revolution* (New York: Dodd, Mead, 1983), p. 348.

11. Harold Nicolson, *Diaries and Letters,* vol. 2, *The War Years* (New York: Atheneum, 1967), p. 37.

12. C. P. Snow, *Variety of Men* (New York: Scribner, 1966), pp. 149–150.

13. Stephen Skowronek, *The Politics Presidents Make: Leadership from John Adams to George Bush* (Cambridge, Mass.: Belknap Press, 1993), p. 17.

14. Alexander Pope, "Essay on Criticism," in E. Audra and Aubrey Williams (eds.), *Alexander Pope: Pastoral Poetry and an Essay on Criticism* (London: Methuen, 1961), pp. 395–396.

15. Joanna Waley-Cohen, *The Sextants of Beijing: Global Currents in Chinese History* (New York: Norton, 1999), p. 110.

16. William McNeill, *Venice* (Chicago: University of Chicago Press, 1974), p. xv.

17. Johann Goethe, *Faust,* trans. C. F. MacIntyre (New York: New Directions, 1957), pp. 13–14.

18. As quoted in D. W. Meinig, *The Shaping of America: A Geographical Perspective of 500 Years of History,* vol. 2, *Continental America, 1800–1867* (New Haven, Conn.: Yale University Press, 1993), p. 237.

19. There are many useful discussions of the distinctions among logos, pathos, and ethos. See, for example, Edward P. J. Corbett, *Classical Rhetoric for the Modern Student*, 3rd ed. (New York: Oxford University Press, 1990), pp. 37–94.

20. James Boswell, *Life of Johnson*, rev. ed., ed. R. W. Chapman (Oxford: Oxford University Press, 1970), Apr. 3, 1773, p. 509.

21. Edgar Lustgarten, "The Trial of Lizzie Borden," in Ephraim London (ed.), *The World of Law*, vol. 2, *The Law as Literature* (New York: Simon & Schuster, 1960), p. 295.

22. See Doris Kearns, *Lyndon Johnson and the American Dream* (New York: Signet, 1977), pp. 171–172; and Robert Dallek, *Flawed Giant: Lyndon Johnson and His Times, 1961–1973* (New York: Oxford University Press, 1988), p. 8.

23. For a compelling description of Johnson's persuasive techniques, see Kearns, *Lyndon Johnson and the American Dream*, pp. 127–130, along with Dallek, *Flawed Giant*, pp. 473–478.

24. Plato, *Philebus*, 58b, in Edith Hamilton and Huntington Cairns (eds.), *Plato: The Collected Dialogues*, trans. R. Hackforth (Princeton, N.J.: Princeton University Press, 1963).

25. Tacitus, *Agricola*, 30, trans. William Peterson (London: William Heinemann, 1925).

26. Samuel Johnson, *A Journey to the Western Islands of Scotland*, ed. R. W. Chapman (Oxford: Oxford University Press, 1970), p. 88.

27. Edmund Burke, "On Conciliation with the Colonies," in Hugh Law (ed.), *Edmund Burke: Speeches and Letters on American Affairs* (1908; New York: Dutton, 1956), p. 89.

28. James Boyd White, *When Words Lose Their Meaning: Constitutions and Reconstitutions of Language, Character, and Community* (Chicago: University of Chicago Press, 1984), p. 37.

29. Alfred North Whitehead, *Adventures of Ideas* (New York: Macmillan, 1933), pp. 105–106.

30. Marcel Mauss, *The Gift: Forms and Functions of Exchange in Archaic Societies*, trans. Ian Cunnison (New York: Norton, 1967), p. 80.

31. Ivone Kirkpatrick, *Mussolini: A Study in Power* (New York: Hawthorn Books, 1964), facing p. 289.

32. As quoted in *New York Times*, June 16, 1934, p. 2.

33. John Angus Campbell, "Charles Darwin: Rhetorician of Science," in John S. Nelson, Allan Megill, and Donald N. McCloskey (eds.), *The Rhetoric of the Human Sciences: Language and Argument in Scholarship and Public Affairs* (Madison: University of Wisconsin Press, 1987), p. 69.

34. Campbell, "Charles Darwin," p. 76.

35. Philip J. Davis and Reuben Hersh, "Rhetoric and Mathematics," in Nelson, Megill, and McCloskey (eds.), *The Rhetoric of the Human Sciences*, pp. 60, 68.

36. Donald N. McCloskey, *The Rhetoric of Economics* (Madison: University of Wisconsin Press, 1985), p. 16. See also Arjo Klamer, "As If Economists and Their Subject Were Rational," in Nelson, Megill, and McCloskey (eds.), *The Rhetoric of the Human Sciences*, pp. 163–183.

37. As cited in Donald N. McCloskey, *Knowledge and Persuasion in Economics* (Cambridge: Cambridge University Press, 1994), p. 39.

38. Renato Rosaldo, "Where Objectivity Lies: The Rhetoric of Anthropology," in Nelson, Megill, and McCloskey (eds.), *The Rhetoric of the Human Sciences*, p. 88. An interesting title, what with the play on words.

39. Clifford Geertz, *Works and Lives: The Anthropologist as Author* (Stanford, Calif.: Stanford University Press, 1988), p. 10.

40. Morris R. Cohen, *The Meaning of Human History* (LaSalle, Ill.: Open Court, 1947), p. 34.

41. Peter Gay, *Style in History* (New York: McGraw-Hill, 1974). And along these lines, see Allen Megill and Donald N. McCloskey, "The Rhetoric of History," in Nelson, Megill, and McCloskey (eds.), *The Rhetoric of the Human Sciences*, pp. 221–238. More generally, see Brian Fay, Eugene O. Golub, and Richard T. Vann (eds.), *Louis O. Mink: Historical Understanding* (Ithaca, N.Y.: Cornell University Press, 1987).

42. David P. Jordan, *Gibbon and His Roman Empire* (Urbana: University of Illinois Press, 1971), p. 18.

43. Jordan, *Gibbon and His Roman Empire*, p. 19.

44. White, *When Words Lose Their Meaning*, p. 273. I continue to be grateful for White's astonishing and persuasive insights. In addition to many useful essays in *When Words Lose Their Meaning*, see his *The Legal Imagination*, abridged ed. (Chicago: University of Chicago Press, 1985); *Heracles' Bow: Essays on the Rhetoric and Poetics of the Law* (Madison: University of Wisconsin Press, 1985); *Justice as Translation: An Essay in Cultural and Legal Criticism* (Chicago: University of Chicago Press, 1990); and *Acts of Hope: Creating Authority in Literature, Law, and Politics* (Chicago: University of Chicago Press, 1994).

45. See, for example, relevant chapters in Nelson, Megill, and McCloskey (eds.), *The Rhetoric of the Human Sciences*.

46. Arthur Quiller-Couch, *On the Art of Writing* (New York: Putnam, 1916), pp. 42–43.

47. Plato, *Gorgias*, 503–504, trans. Walter Hamilton (Harmondsworth, U.K.: Penguin Books, 1971).

48. Cicero, *De Oratore*, III, 60, 61.

49. Cicero, *De Oratore*, III, 56.

50. John Dewey, *Reconstruction in Philosophy*, enl. ed. (Boston: Beacon Press, 1948), pp. 30–32. For further discussion of Bacon's approach to rhetoric, see Brian Vickers, "Bacon and Rhetoric," in Markku Peltonen (ed.), *The Cambridge Companion to Bacon* (Cambridge: Cambridge University Press, 1996), pp. 200–231.

51. Aristotle, *Rhetoric* 1355b, trans. John Henry Freese (Cambridge, Mass.: Harvard University Press, 1982).

52. "What They Were Thinking," *New York Times Magazine*, Aug. 27, 2000, p. 26.

53. Robert L. Heilbroner, *Business Civilization in Decline* (New York: Norton, 1976), pp. 113-114.

54. Vance Packard, *The Hidden Persuaders* (New York: McKay, 1957); William H. Whyte, *The Organization Man* (New York: Simon &

Schuster, 1956); David Riesman in collaboration with Reuel Denney and Nathan Glazer, *The Lonely Crowd: A Study of the Changing American Character* (New Haven, Conn.: Yale University Press, 1950); Michael Schudson, *Advertising, The Uneasy Persuasion: Its Dubious Impact on American Society* (New York: Basic Books, 1984).

55. For just a small sampling of American politics in decline, see E. J. Dionne, Jr., *Why Americans Hate Politics* (New York: Simon & Schuster, 1991); Kevin Phillips, *Arrogant Capital* (Boston: Little, Brown, 1994); William Greider, *Who Will Tell the People: The Betrayal of American Democracy* (New York: Simon & Schuster, 1992); Jonathan Rauch, *Demosclerosis: The Silent Killer of American Government* (New York: Times Books, 1994); and Robert Parry, *Fooling America: How Washington Insiders Twist the Truth and Manufacture the Conventional Wisdom* (New York: Morrow, 1992).

56. See Garry Wills, *Lincoln at Gettysburg: The Words That Remade America* (New York: Simon & Schuster, 1992).

57. See, for example, Shelley Ross, *Fall from Grace: Sex, Scandal, and Corruption in American Politics from 1702 to the Present* (New York: Ballantine, 1988).

58. Cicero, *De Oratore*, III, 60.

59. William Shakespeare, *The Winter's Tale* (London: Routledge, 1986), 5.2.

Chapter Two

1. Gregory Bateson, *Steps to an Ecology of Mind* (New York: Ballantine, 1972; reissued with an introduction by Mary Catherine Bateson, Chicago: University of Chicago Press, 2000), p. 494.

2. Niccolo Machiavelli, *The Prince*, trans. Harvey C. Mansfield, Jr. (Chicago: University of Chicago Press, 1985), Chap. 23, pp. 94–95.

3. It is not too much of a stretch to consider information seeking and, in particular, devious information seeking, as a theme running throughout *Hamlet*. The first words of the play give us a clue: "Who's there?" is the query from Barnardo, a sentinel on duty.

In the course of the ensuing action, Hamlet seeks information from his father and has to determine whether the information is trustworthy; Polonius sets a spy on his son; Polonius hangs around the corridors trying to seek information from Hamlet; Polonius sets his daughter as a spy on Hamlet; Claudius has Rosencrantz and Guildenstern spy on Hamlet; Polonius hides in Gertrude's bedroom to spy on Hamlet.

4. Thomas Cleary (ed. and trans.), *Zen Lessons: The Art of Leadership* (Boston: Shambhala, 1989), pp. 85–86.

5. Plato, *Laches,* 178b, in Edith Hamilton and Huntington Cairns (eds.), *Plato: The Collected Dialogues,* trans. Benjamin Jowett (Princeton, N.J.: Princeton University Press, 1963).

6. William Shakespeare, *Julius Caesar* (London: Methuen, 1972), 4.3.

7. Francis Bacon, "Of Simulation and Dissimulation," in *The Essays,* ed. John Pitcher (London: Penguin Books, 1985), p. 76.

8. Benjamin Franklin, *Autobiography,* in J. A. Leo Lemay (ed.), *Writings* (New York: Library of America, 1987), p. 1385.

9. Lord Chesterfield, *Letters, Sentences and Maxims* (London: Chesterfield Society, 1910), p. 333.

10. Sinclair Lewis, *Elmer Gantry* (New York: New American Library, 1970), p. 88.

11. See David Nyberg, *The Varnished Truth: Truth Telling and Deceiving in Ordinary Life* (Chicago: University of Chicago Press, 1993), pp. 137–153; see also Sisella Bok, *Lying: Moral Choice in Public and Private Life* (New York: Vintage Books, 1989).

12. Machiavelli, *The Prince,* Chap. 23.

13. William Shakespeare, *Macbeth* (London: Methuen, 1986), 5.1.

14. *Macbeth,* 5.3.

15. Francis Bacon, *De Sapienta Veterum,* VIII, Endymion; or the favourite, in James Spedding, Robert Ellis, and Douglas Heath (eds.), *The Works of Francis Bacon* (London: Longman, 1858), p. 717.

16. William Shakespeare, *Julius Caesar* (London: Methuen, 1972), 1.2.

17. Confucius, *Analects*, 14.22, trans. Simon Leys (New York: Norton, 1997), p. 70.

18. Machiavelli, *The Prince*, Chap. 23.

19. Paul Johnson, *Elizabeth I* (New York: Holt, Rinehart and Winston, 1974), p. 65.

20. Augustine, *Confessions* X:23, trans. F. J. Sheed (Indianapolis, Ind.: Hackett, 1993), p. 190.

21. For a useful discussion of self-deception, see Nyberg, *The Varnished Truth*, pp. 81–108.

22. Johnson, *Elizabeth I*, p. 283.

23. Plutarch, "Marcus Brutus," in *The Lives of the Noble Grecians and Romans*, trans. John Dryden (New York: Modern Library, n.d.), p. 1192.

24. Barbara Tuchman, *The March of Folly: From Troy to Vietnam* (New York: Knopf, 1984).

25. Irving L. Janis, *Groupthink: Psychological Studies of Policy Decisions and Fiascoes*, 2nd ed. (Boston: Houghton Mifflin, 1972), p. 119. See also Robert Dallek, *Flawed Giant: Lyndon Johnson and His Times, 1961–1973* (New York: Oxford University Press, 1998), Chaps. 7–9.

26. Thomas Cleary (ed. and trans.), *The Book of Leadership and Strategy: Lessons of the Chinese Masters* (Boston: Shambhala, 1992), p. 41.

27. Machiavelli, *The Prince*, Chap. 23.

28. Lord Chesterfield to his son, Jan. 15, 1753, in Bonamy Dobrée (ed.), *The Letters of Philip Dormer Stanhope, 4th Earl of Chesterfield* (New York: Viking, 1932), 5:1996.

29. *The Letters of the Younger Pliny*, trans. Betty Radice (New York: Penguin Books, 1963), Book 10, No. 97, p. 295.

30. Marquis de Custine, *Journey for Our Time: The Russian Journals of the Marquis de Custine* (Washington, D.C.: Regnery, 1987), p. 50.

31. Shakespeare, *Hamlet*, 2.1. It is unfortunate that this scene is often cut from stage and film productions because it underscores the role of information seeking in the play, as well as foreshadows the later machinations of the clever Polonius and the results of such cleverness.

32. Lord Chesterfield to his son, Jan. 15, 1753, in Dobrée (ed.), *The Letters of Philip Dormer Stanhope, 4th Earl of Chesterfield,* pp. 1996–1997.

33. James Boswell, *Life of Johnson* (Oxford: Oxford University Press, 1980), p. 188.

34. Francis Bacon, "Of Cunning," in *The Essays,* p. 127.

35. Bacon, "Of Cunning," p. 128.

36. Bacon, "Of Simulation and Dissimulation," in *The Essays,* p. 78.

37. Michel de Montaigne, "Of Presumption," in *The Complete Essays of Montaigne,* trans. Donald M. Frame (Stanford, Calif.: Stanford University Press, 1958), p. 491.

38. Marcel Mauss, *The Gift: Forms and Functions of Exchange in Archaic Societies,* trans. Ian Cunnison (New York: Norton, 1967), esp. Chap. 1, and, for a discussion of the potlatch, Chap. 2.

39. Peter Blau, *Exchange and Power in Social Life* (New York: Wiley, 1964), p. 94.

40. Lord Chesterfield, *Letters, Sentences and Maxims,* p. 328.

41. Tacitus, *Annals,* I,11, trans. Michael Grant (New York: Penguin Books, 1977), p. 39.

42. Stendhal, *Lucien Leuwen,* trans. H.L.R. Edwards (New York: Penguin Books, 1991), p. 276.

43. Montaigne, "On the Art of Discussion," in *The Complete Essays,* p. 718.

44. William Gibson, *Shakespeare's Game* (New York: Atheneum, 1978), pp. 9–10.

45. For a description of the cracking of the German codes, see John Keegan, *World War II* (New York: Penguin Books, 1989), pp. 499ff. See also Simon Singh, *The Code Breakers* (New York: Doubleday, 1999), pp. 143–189, as well as David Kahn's very useful *The Race to Break the German U-Boat Codes, 1939–1943* (Boston: Houghton Mifflin, 1991).

46. Martin Gilbert, *The Second World War* (New York: Henry Holt, 1989), p. 178. Mary, queen of Scots, also had misplaced confidence

in her codes. In a letter intercepted by Elizabeth's spies, Mary was explicit in her support of the conspiracy against Elizabeth; this "smoking gun" pushed Elizabeth at long last to have Mary executed.

47. Alexis de Tocqueville, *The Old Regime and the French Revolution*, trans. Stuart Gilbert (New York: Doubleday Anchor, 1955), p. 177. Similarly, Frederick Douglass, *Narrative of the Life of Frederick Douglass, an American Slave* (New York: Penguin Books, 1982): "I have observed this in my experience of slavery—that whenever my condition was improved, instead of its increasing my contentment, it only increased my desire to be free, and set me to thinking of plans to gain my freedom" (p. 135).

48. Richard Breitman, *Official Secrets: What the Nazis Planned, What the British and Americans Knew* (New York: Hill and Wang, 1998).

Chapter Three

1. Aristotle, *Ethics*, 1111b, 1112a, 1113a, trans. J.A.K. Thompson (New York: Penguin Books, 1976).

2. Niccolo Machiavelli, *Discourses*, 1,1, trans. Harvey C. Mansfield and Nathan Tarcov (Chicago: University of Chicago Press, 1996), p. 8.

3. Immanuel Kant, *Groundwork of the Metaphysics of Morals*, trans. Mary J. Gregor (Cambridge: Cambridge University Press, 1996), p. 95.

4. William James, *The Principles of Psychology* (New York: Henry Holt, 1899), 1:287–288.

5. Michel de Montaigne, "On Vanity," in *The Complete Essays of Montaigne*, trans. Donald M. Frame (Stanford, Calif.: Stanford University Press, 1958), p. 739.

6. John Dewey, "Philosophies of Freedom," in Jo Ann Boydston (ed.), *John Dewey: The Later Works, 1925–1953*, vol. 3, *1927–1928* (Carbondale: Southern Illinois University Press, 1984), p. 104.

7. Aristotle, *Rhetoric*, 1355b, trans. W. Rhys Roberts (New York: Modern Library, 1954).

8. Francis Bacon, *The Advancement of Learning* (London: Dent, 1973), p. 146.

9. Richard Weaver, "Language Is Sermonic," in Richard L. Johannesen, Rennard Strickland, and Ralph T. Eubanks (eds.), *Language Is Sermonic: Richard M. Weaver on the Nature of Rhetoric* (Baton Rouge: Louisiana State University Press, 1970), p. 211.

10. Richard Weaver to Ralph T. Eubanks, Jan. 19, 1961, quoted in Johannesen, Strickland, and Eubanks (eds.), *Language Is Sermonic*, p. 56.

11. Richard Weaver, *The Ethics of Rhetoric* (Washington, D.C.: Regnery, 1953), p. 24.

12. Walter H. Beale, "Richard M. Weaver: Philosophical Rhetoric, Cultural Criticism, and the First Rhetorical Awakening," *College English* 52, 6 (Oct. 1990): 626.

13. P. Albert Duhamel, "The Function of Rhetoric as Effective Expression," *Journal of the History of Ideas* 10, 3 (June 1949): 345.

14. Albert Camus, *The Rebel: An Essay on Man in Revolt*, trans. Anthony Bower (New York: Vintage Books, 1991), p. 57.

15. Aristotle, *Rhetoric*, 1357a.

16. For a useful summary, see Edward P. J. Corbett, *Classical Rhetoric for the Modern Student*, 3rd ed. (New York: Oxford University Press, 1990).

17. James Madison, Federalist No. 10 and Federalist No. 51, in Garry Wills (ed.), *The Federalist Papers by Alexander Hamilton, James Madison, and John Jay* (New York: Bantam Books, 1982), pp. 44, 262.

18. Weaver, *Ethics of Rhetoric*, p. 56.

19. Roger Soder, "The Rhetoric of Teacher Professionalization," in John I. Goodlad, Roger Soder, and Kenneth A. Sirotnik (eds.), *The Moral Dimensions of Teaching* (San Francisco: Jossey-Bass, 1990), pp. 35–86.

20. Weaver, *Ethics of Rhetoric*, pp. 58, 84, 114.

21. Winston Churchill, Mar. 1936, speech at the Conservative Members Committee on Foreign Affairs Meeting, London, in Robert Rhodes James (ed.), *Winston S. Churchill: His Complete Speeches, 1897–1963*, vol. 6, *1935–1942* (New York: Bowker, 1974), p. 5694.

22. Tocqueville, *Democracy in America*, Vol. 1, Part II, Chap. 2, trans. Harvey C. Mansfield and Delba Winthrop (Chicago: University of Chicago Press, 2000), p. 167.

23. Weaver, *Ethics of Rhetoric*, p. 76. Here we are perhaps close to Proverbs: "Where there is no vision, the people perish."

24. There are those who raise questions about Weaver's argument, especially regarding his characterization of Burke as a liberal given Burke's habitual rhetorical grounding. See, for example, Dennis R. Bormann, "The 'Uncontested Term' Contested: An Analysis of Weaver on Burke," *Quarterly Journal of Speech* 57, 3 (Oct. 1971): 298–305; Richard L. Johannesen, "Richard M. Weaver on Standards for Ethical Rhetoric," *Central States Speech Journal* 29 (Summer 1978): 127–135; John R. E. Bliese, "Richard Weaver's Axiology of Argument," *Southern Speech Communication Journal* 44 (Spring 1979): 275–288; and J. Michael Sproule, "Using Public Rhetoric to Assess Private Philosophy: Richard M. Weaver and Beyond," *Southern Speech Communication Journal* 44 (Spring 1979): 289–308.

25. Ingmar Bergman, *Four Plays of Ingmar Bergman*, trans. Lars Malmstrom and David Kushner (New York: Simon & Schuster, 1960), pp. 79, 237.

26. Barbara W. Tuchman, *The March of Folly: From Troy to Vietnam* (New York: Knopf, 1984).

27. James Boyd White, *When Words Lose Their Meaning: Constitutions and Reconstitutions of Language, Character, and Community* (Chicago: University of Chicago Press, 1984), p. 93.

28. Edmund Burke, "Thoughts on the Present Discontents," in B. W. Hill (ed.), *Edmund Burke on Government, Politics and Society* (London: Fontana, 1975), p. 76.

29. Johann Wolfgang von Goethe, *Goethe's Poems and Aphorisms*, ed. Friedrich Burns (New York: Oxford University Press, 1936), p. 16.

30. James Boswell, *Life of Samuel Johnson* (New York: Modern Library, 1952), p. 212.

31. Alfred North Whitehead, *Adventures of Ideas* (New York: Macmillan, 1933), p. 84.

32. Warren Hoge, "Murdoch Halts a Book Critical of China," *New York Times*, Feb. 28, 1998, p. A5.

33. Tillie Olsen, "One out of Twelve: Writers Who Are Women in Our Century," in Tillie Olsen, *Silences* (New York: Delta, 1978), p. 40.

34. Weaver, *Language Is Sermonic*, pp. 192–193.

35. Plato, *Cratylus*, 388c, in Edith Hamilton and Huntington Cairns (eds.), *Plato: The Collected Dialogues*, trans. Benjamin Jowett (Princeton, N.J.: Princeton University Press, 1963), p. 426.

36. Lewis Carroll, *Through the Looking Glass* (New York: Collier, 1962), p. 247.

37. Wendell Berry, *Standing by Words* (San Francisco: North Point, 1983), pp. 24, 25.

38. Berry, *Standing by Words*, p. 55.

39. Tocqueville, *Democracy in America*, Vol. 2, Part 1.

40. Martin Gilbert, *Finest Hour: Winston S. Churchill, 1939–1941*, vol. 6, *The Churchill Biography* (Portsmouth, N.H.: Heinemann, 1983), pp. 600–601.

41. *Seattle Times*, July 2, 1993, p. B2.

42. ABCNEWS.com @www.abcnews.go.com/sections/us/DailyNews/beaver001120.html.

43. Thucydides, *The Peloponnesian War*, 3.82, trans. Richard Crawley (New York: Modern Library, 1951).

44. George Orwell, "Politics and the English Language," in Sonia Orwell and Ian Angos (eds.), *The Collected Essays, Journalism and Letters of George Orwell* (New York: Harcourt Brace Jovanovich 1968), 4:136–137. For many illuminating and depressing examples of euphemism, see William Lutz, *Doublespeak* (New York: Harper & Row, 1989), and Lutz, *The New Doublespeak* (New York:

HarperCollins, 1996). See also Peter Burke and Roy Porter (eds.), *Languages and Jargons: Contributions to a Social History of Language* (Cambridge, U.K.: Polity Press, 1995); Mario Pei, *Doublespeak in America* (New York: Hawthorn, 1973); Keith Allan and Kate Burridge, *Euphemism and Dysphemism: Language Used as Shield and Weapon* (New York: Oxford University Press, 1991); and D. J. Enright (ed.), *Fair of Speech: The Uses of Euphemism* (New York: Oxford University Press, 1985).

45. Lope de Vega, "Fuenteovejuna," in *Lope de Vega: Five Plays*, trans. Jill Booty (New York: Hill and Wang, 1961), p. 64.

46. Günter Grass, *Dog Years* (New York: Harcourt, Brace & World, 1965), p. 346.

47. Richard Pipes, *Russia Under the Bolshevik Regime* (New York: Knopf, 1993), p. 327.

48. Camus, *The Rebel*, p. 250.

49. Mihail Sebastian, *Journal 1935–1944: The Fascist Years*, trans. Patrick Camiller (Chicago: Ivan Dee, 2000), p. 334.

50. Jung Chang, *Wild Swans: Three Daughters of China* (New York: Doubleday, 1991), p. 225.

51. Tocqueville, *Democracy in America*, Vol. 2, Part 1, Chap. 16, p. 454.

52. Jonathan Glover, *Humanity: A Moral History of the Twentieth Century* (New Haven, Conn.: Yale University Press, 2000), p. 37. There are many examples of distancing language in this depressing volume, drawn from, for example, the Bolshevik Revolution, Hitler and the Nazis, and the Cultural Revolution in China.

53. Melvin Konner, *Becoming a Doctor: A Journey of Initiation in Medical School* (New York: Viking, 1987), pp. 379, 382, 384.

54. Richard A. Lanham, *Style: An Anti-Textbook* (New Haven, Conn.: Yale University Press, 1974). See especially Chap. 2.

55. Orwell, "Politics and the English Language," p. 138.

56. Corbett, *Classical Rhetoric for the Modern Student*, p. 402.

57. Weaver, *The Ethics of Rhetoric*, p. 121.

58. Lord Chesterfield to his son, Dec. 9, O.S. 1749, in Bonamy Dobrée (ed.), *The Letters of Philip Dormer Stanhope, 4th Earl of Chesterfield* (New York: Viking, 1932), 4:1458.

59. Arthur Quiller-Couch, *On the Art of Writing* (New York: Putnam, 1916), pp. 292–293.

60. Albert J. Beveridge, *Abraham Lincoln: 1809–1858* (Boston: Houghton Mifflin, 1928), 1:134.

61. Richard L. Johannesen, "Attitude of Speaker Toward Audience: A Significant Concept for Contemporary Rhetorical Theory and Criticism," *Central States Speech Journal* 25, 2 (Summer 1974): 95.

62. James Boyd White, *The Legal Imagination*, abridged ed. (Chicago: University of Chicago Press, 1985), p. 1.

63. Gregory Bateson, *Steps to an Ecology of Mind* (New York: Ballantine, 1972; reissued with an introduction by Mary Catherine Bateson, Chicago: University of Chicago Press, 2000), p. 492.

64. Bateson, *Steps to an Ecology of Mind*, p. 512.

65. Mary Ann Glendon, *Rights Talk: The Impoverishment of Political Discourse* (New York: Free Press, 1991), p. xi.

66. Michael Ignatieff, *The Needs of Strangers* (New York: Viking Penguin, 1984), p. 142.

67. Dewey, "Philosophies of Freedom," p. 113.

68. Orwell, "The Principles of Newspeak," appendix to *1984* (New York: New American Library, 1961), p. 246.

69. Glendon, *Rights Talk*, p. 173.

70. Primo Levi, "On Obscure Writing," in *Other People's Trades*, trans. Raymond Rosenthal (New York: Summit Books, 1989), p. 174.

71. Richard Weaver, "Reflections of Modernity," in Richard Weaver, *Life Without Prejudice, and Other Essays* (Chicago: Regnery, 1965), p. 118.

72. Jeff Shesol, *Mutual Contempt: Lyndon Johnson, Robert Kennedy, and the Feud That Defined a Decade* (New York: Norton, 1997), p. 309.

73. Albert R. Hunt, "Verbal Violence Begets Physical Violence," *Wall Street Journal*, Nov. 9, 1995, p. A23.

74. As quoted by Rollo May, *Power and Innocence: A Search for the Sources of Violence* (New York: Norton, 1972), p. 65.

75. Alexander Hamilton, Federalist No. 1, in Garry Wills (ed.), *The Federalist Papers by Alexander Hamilton, James Madison, and John Jay* (New York: Bantam Books, 1982), p. 3.

76. Max Schulz, "King Weasel," *American Spectator* (Oct. 2000): 45, 46.

77. Ben Jonson, "Explorata: or Discoveries," in George Parfitt (ed.), *The Complete Poems of Ben Jonson* (New Haven, Conn.: Yale University Press, 1975), p. 435.

Chapter Four

1. Robert Conquest, *We and They* (London: Temple Smith, 1980), p. 12.

2. Conquest, *We and They,* p. 15.

3. Herbert J. Muller, *The Uses of the Past: Profiles of Former Societies* (New York: Oxford University Press, 1957), p. 71. For Popper's discussion of the differences between closed and open societies, see *The Open Society and Its Enemies* (Princeton, N.J.: Princeton University Press, 1950).

4. Robert A. Dahl, *Democracy and Its Critics* (New Haven, Conn.: Yale University Press, 1989) p. 221.

5. Adrian Karatnycky, "The 1999 Freedom House Survey: A Century of Progress," *Journal of Democracy* 11, 1 (Jan. 2000): 188.

6. Freedom House, *Freedom in the World: The Annual Survey of Political Rights and Civil Liberties, 1999–2000* (New York: Freedom House, 2000).

7. Ralph Lerner, *The Thinking Revolutionary: Principle and Practice in the New Republic* (Ithaca, N.Y.: Cornell University Press, 1987), p. 61.

8. Some readers may wonder why I am emphasizing hawks from handsaws and why it is important to make distinctions. I do so because some people profess to see no real difference between despotic cultures and democratic civic cultures, between oppression and freedom. For some, the mere existence of some sort of oppression anywhere within a democratic civic culture is enough to taint the

whole and to make that culture no better (and possibly even worse) than a despotic culture. I am not among those who claim to see no differences.

9. Alexis de Tocqueville, *Democracy in America,* Vol. I, Part 2, Chap. 10, trans. Harvey C. Mansfield and Delba Winthrop (Chicago: University of Chicago Press, 2000), pp. 396–397.

10. Martin Malia, for example, finds Custine "shrill" and a perpetrator of the notion that internal despotism inevitably spawns external aggression. See Malia's *Russia Under Western Eyes: From the Bronze Horseman to the Lenin Mausoleum* (Cambridge, Mass.: Belknap Press, 1999), pp. 98–99. Others regard Custine more positively. George F. Kennan, for example, concludes that "whichever of his many weaknesses which may be held against him, his readers of the present age must concede that he detected . . . traits in the mentality of Russian government, some active, some latent, the recognition and correction of which would be vital to the future success and security of Russian society—to its security, above all, not just against those external forces by whose fancied heretical will Russians of all ages have so easily seen themselves threatened, but rather its security against itself." George F. Kennan, *The Marquis de Custine and His Russia in 1839* (Princeton, N.J.: Princeton University Press, 1971), p. 131.

11. Marquis de Custine, *Journey for Our Time: The Russian Journals of the Marquis de Custine* (Washington, D.C.: Regnery, 1987), pp. 99–100.

12. Custine, *Journey for Our Time,* pp. 350; 112.

13. "Cult's Followers Rally in Beijing," *New York Times,* Apr. 26, 1999, p. A1.

14. Custine, *Journey for Our Time,* pp. 158–159.

15. There is no room here to note even a portion of the important literature on the Soviet totalitarian regime and its evils. At a minimum, one would want to consult Richard Pipes (ed.), *The Unknown Lenin: From the Secret Archive* (New Haven, Conn.: Yale University Press, 1996), along with Robert Conquest's many valuable works,

including *The Great Terror: A Reassessment* (New York: Oxford University Press, 1990); *The Harvest of Sorrow: Soviet Collectivization and the Terror-Famine* (New York: Oxford University Press, 1986); and *Reflections on a Ravaged Century* (New York: Norton, 2000). Also of major importance is Richard Pipes's *Russia Under the Bolshevik Regime* (New York: Knopf, 1993), along with Stéphane Courtois and others, *The Black Book of Communism*, trans. Jonathan Murphy and Mark Kramer (Cambridge, Mass.: Harvard University Press, 1999) and François Furet, *The Passing of an Illusion: The Idea of Communism in the Twentieth Century*, trans. Deborah Furet (Chicago: University of Chicago Press, 1999). Of the many personal accounts of life in the totalitarian regime, one particularly compelling to me is Eugene Ginzberg, *Within the Whirlwind*, trans. Ian Boland (New York: Harcourt Brace Jovanovich, 1981).

16. Custine, *Journey for Our Time*, p. 372.

17. See Solomon Volkov, *St. Petersburg: A Cultural History* (New York: Free Press, 1995), p. 477.

18. For a frightening summary of the atrocities of the twentieth century, see Jonathan Glover, *Humanity: A Moral History of the Twentieth Century* (New Haven, Conn.: Yale University Press, 2000).

19. "Democracy in Russia: How Free Is Free?" *Economist*, Nov. 25, 2000, p. 26.

20. *Tao Te Ching*, no. 58, in *The Essential Tao*, trans. Thomas Cleary (San Francisco: HarperCollins, 1993).

21. Gustave E. Grunebaum, *Medieval Islam*, 2nd ed. (Chicago: University of Chicago Press, 1954), p. 250, n. 67.

22. Alexander Pushkin, "The Bronze Horseman," in *Narrative Poems by Alexander Pushkin and Michael Lermontov*, trans. Charles Johnston (New York: Random House, 1983), pp. 38, 53. For commentary, see Waclaw Lednicki, *Pushkin's Bronze Horseman: The Story of a Masterpiece* (Berkeley: University of California Press, 1955); see also Volkov, *St. Petersburg*, pp. 3–25.

23. Sheila Fitzpatrick, *Everyday Stalinism: Ordinary Life in Extraordinary Times: Soviet Russia in the 1930s* (New York: Oxford University

Press, 1999), p. 222. Another way to deal with a continuing stream of orders from on high is to follow them as precisely as possible. The archetype in literature here is Jaroslav Hasek's *The Good Soldier: Schweik*, a wonderful portrait of a soldier who continually throws the military system into confusion simply by following all orders literally. For a useful discussion of compliance behavior as a function of coercive institutions, see Amitai Etzioni, *A Comparative Analysis of Complex Organizations*, rev. and enl. ed. (New York: Free Press, 1975). See also Amitai Etzioni, *The Active Society: A Theory of Societal and Political Processes* (New York: Free Press, 1968), pp. 357–381.

24. Andrew Nagorski, *The Birth of Freedom: Shaping Lives and Societies in Eastern Europe* (New York: Simon & Schuster, 1993), p. 54.

25. William Shakespeare, *Richard II* (London: Methuen, 1961), 5.1.

26. On the East German secret police, or Stasi, see Timothy Garton Ash, *The File: A Personal History* (New York: Random House, 1997), and David Childs and Richard Popplewell, *The Stasi: The East German Intelligence and Security Service* (New York: New York University Press, 1996).

27. See Francis Fukuyama, *The End of History and the Last Man* (New York: Free Press, 1992). See also Jean-François Revel, "But We Follow the Worse . . . ," *National Interest*, no. 18 (Winter 1989–1990): 99.

28. Thucydides, *The Peloponnesian War*, II: 39–40, trans. Richard Crawley (New York: Modern Library, 1951), pp. 104–105.

29. George Wilson Pierson, *Tocqueville in America* (1938; Baltimore, Md.: Johns Hopkins University Press, 1996), p. 588.

30. Daniel Boorstin, *Cleopatra's Nose* (New York: Random House, 1994), pp. 63–73.

31. See, for example, the twenty-four hundred pages of documents superbly edited by Bernard Bailyn in *The Debate on the Constitution: Federalist and Antifederalist Speeches, Articles, and Letters During the Struggle over Ratification, Part One: September 1787 to February 1788* and *Part Two: January to August 1788* (New York: Library of America, 1993). See also Charles S. Hyneman and Donald S. Lutz (eds.),

American Political Writing During the Founding Era, 1760–1805 (Indianapolis, Ind.: LibertyPress, 1983), and Ellis Sandoz (ed.), *Political Sermons of the American Founding Era, 1730–1805* (Indianapolis, Ind.: LibertyPress, 1991).

32. For an interesting account of a gadfly newspaper in the early United States, see Richard N. Rosenfeld, *American Aurora: A Democratic-Republic Returns* (New York: St. Martin's Press, 1997).

33. See, for example, James Morton Smith, *Freedom's Fetters: The Alien and Sedition Laws and American Civil Liberties* (Ithaca, N.Y.: Cornell University Press, 1956).

34. William Shakespeare, *Richard III*, ed. Antony Hammond (London: Methuen, 1981), 1.4., pp. 170–177.

35. Pipes, *The Unknown Lenin*, p. 50.

36. Robert Nisbet, *The Present Age: Progess and Anarchy in Modern America* (New York: Harper & Row, 1988), p. 21.

37. Mark Twain, "King Leopold's Soliloquy," in Mark Twain: *Following the Equator and Anti-Imperialist Essays* (New York: Oxford University Press, 1996). See also Adam Hochschild, *King Leopold's Ghost* (Boston: Houghton Mifflin, 1998), p. 242.

38. For Sartre's position, see Malia, *Russia Under Western Eyes*, pp. 366–367, as well as Conquest, *Reflections on a Ravaged Century*, p. 137. For a general discussion of Sartre, other French intellectuals, and communism, see Tony Judt, *Past Imperfect: French Intellectuals, 1944–1956* (Berkeley: University of California Press, 1992), and Judt, *The Burden of Responsibility: Blum, Camus, Aron, and the French Twentieth Century* (Chicago: University of Chicago Press, 1998).

39. As quoted in Robert Conquest, *Stalin: Breaker of Nations* (New York: Viking, 1991), p. 214.

40. Ralph Lerner, *Revolutions Revisited: Two Faces of the Politics of Enlightenment* (Chapel Hill: University of North Carolina Press, 1994), p. 59.

41. Lerner, *Revolutions Revisited*, p. 67.

42. Tocqueville to John Stuart Mill, Mar. 18, 1841, in Roger Bask (ed.), *Selected Letters on Politics and Society*, trans. James Taipan and Roger Bask (Berkeley: University of California Press, 1985), pp. 150–151.

43. An earlier version of these conditions is presented in Roger Soder, "Education for Democracy: The Foundation for Democratic Character," in Roger Soder, John I. Goodlad, and Timothy J. McMannon (eds.), *Developing Democratic Character in the Young* (San Francisco: Jossey-Bass, 2001).

44. Of the extensive literature on trust, the following have been particularly useful to me: Diego Gambetta (ed.), *Trust: Making and Breaking Cooperative Relations* (New York: Blackwell, 1988). See also Francis Fukuyama, *Trust: The Social Virtues and the Creation of Prosperity* (New York: Free Press, 1995), as well as his *The Great Disruption: Human Nature and the Reconstitution of Social Order* (New York: Free Press, 1999); Adam B. Seligman, *The Problem of Trust* (Princeton, N.J.: Princeton University Press, 1997); Barbara A. Misztal, *Trust in Modern Societies: The Search for the Bases of Social Order* (Cambridge, U.K.: Polity Press, 1996); and Bernard Barber, *The Logic and Limits of Trust* (New Brunswick, N.J.: Rutgers University Press, 1983).

45. On exchange, see Peter Blau, *Exchange and Power in Social Life* (New York: Wiley, 1964); Marcel Mauss, *The Gift: Forms and Functions of Exchange in Archaic Societies*, trans. Ian Cunnison (New York: Norton, 1967); John Davis, *Exchange* (Buckingham: Open University Press, 1992); and Alfred North Whitehead, *Adventures of Ideas* (New York: Free Press, 1967), Chap. 5.

46. In *Making Democracy Work: Civic Traditions in Modern Italy* (Princeton, N.J.: Princeton University Press, 1993), Robert Putnam and his colleagues argue that the three conditions so far stated (trust, exchange, and social capital) are critical to a healthy democracy. For additional considerations of the notion of social capital, see James Coleman, *Foundations of Social Theory* (Cambridge, Mass.: Belknap Press, 1990), pp. 300–321.

47. Useful here is James Boyd White, *The Legal Imagination* (Chicago: University of Chicago Press, 1987), as well as his *Acts of Hope:*

Creating Authority in Literature, Law, and Politics (Chicago: University of Chicago Press, 1994) and *Justice as Translation: An Essay in Cultural and Legal Criticism* (Chicago: University of Chicago Press, 1990).

48. See, among others, Mary Ann Glendon, *Rights Talk: The Impoverishment of Political Discourse* (New York: Free Press, 1991).

49. Of the many texts useful and inspiring, I keep returning to Herbert Muller, *The Uses of the Past* (New York: Oxford University Press, 1952), pp. 45–71.

50. A most useful discussion is found in Philip B. Kurland and Ralph Lerner (eds.), *The Founder's Constitution: Major Themes* (Chicago: University of Chicago Press, 1987), 1:Chap. 14.

51. See Donald Treadgold, *Freedom: A History* (New York: New York University Press, 1990). See also Herbert Muller's trilogy—*Freedom in the Ancient World* (New York: Harper, 1961), *Freedom in the Western World: From the Dark Ages to the Rise of Democracy* (New York: Harper, 1963), and *Freedom in the Modern World* (New York: Harper, 1966)—as well as his *Issues of Freedom: Paradoxes and Promises* (New York: Harper, 1960). Also useful is Orlando Patterson, *Freedom: Freedom in the Making of Western Culture* (New York: Basic Books, 1991); Isaiah Berlin, *Four Essays on Liberty* (Oxford: Oxford University Press, 1968), and Ruth Nanda Anshen (ed.), *Freedom: Its Meaning* (New York: Harcourt, Brace, 1940). For a discussion of the connection between economic freedom and political freedom, see Amartya Sen, *Development as Freedom* (New York: Knopf, 1999). Robert Nisbet's *The Present Age: Progress and Anarchy in Modern America* (New York: Harper & Row, 1988) presents a useful analysis of threats to freedom; see especially Chap. 2 on the growth of invasive government. Also useful for his discussion of threats to freedom by invasive government is James C. Scott's *Seeing Like a State: How Certain Schemes to Improve the Human Condition Have Failed* (New Haven, Conn.: Yale University Press, 1998).

52. Nisbet, *The Present Age*, p. 57.

53. Leo Strauss, *Persecution and the Art of Writing* (1952; Chicago: University of Chicago Press, 1988), p. 37.

54. See Gregory Bateson, *Steps to an Ecology of Mind* (New York: Ballantine, 1972; reissued with an introduction by Mary Catherine Bateson, Chicago: University of Chicago Press, 2000). For an exceedingly useful explication of Bateson's thought, see Peter Harries-Jones, *A Recursive Vision: Ecological Understanding and Gregory Bateson* (Toronto: University of Toronto Press, 1995).

55. Tocqueville, *Democracy in America*, Vol. II, Part 4, Chap. 6, p. 663. See also Nathan Tarcov, "The Meanings of Democracy," in Roger Soder (ed.), *Democracy, Education, and the Schools* (San Francisco: Jossey-Bass, 1996), pp. 1–36.

56. David S. Landes, *The Wealth and Poverty of Nations* (New York: Norton, 1998), p. 520.

57. James Madison, Federalist No. 51, in Garry Wills (ed.), *The Federalist Papers by Alexander Hamilton, James Madison and John Jay* (New York: Bantam Books, 1982), p. 262.

58. For a defense of modern Singapore by its creator, see Lee Kuan Yew, *From Third World to First: The Singapore Story: 1965–2000* (New York: HarperCollins, 2000).

59. Plutarch, *Dion*, in *The Age of Alexander: Nine Greek Lives by Plutarch*, trans. Ian Scott-Kilvert (New York: Penguin Books, 1973), p. 111.

60. Leo Strauss, *What Is Political Philosophy? and Other Studies* (Chicago: University of Chicago Press, 1959), p. 43.

61. Douglas McGregor, *The Human Side of Enterprise* (New York: McGraw-Hill, 1960).

62. Muller, *Freedom in the Western World*, p. 301.

63. See Tarcov, "The Meanings of Democracy."

64. Madison to William T. Barry, Aug. 4, 1822, in Gaillard Hunt (ed.), *The Writings of James Madison* (New York: Putnam, 1900–1910), 9:105.

65. The work of the Center for Educational Renewal at the University of Washington, as well as the related independent Institute for Educational Inquiry, Seattle, has focused on the democracy, education,

and schooling connections. See, for example, John Goodlad, *Educational Renewal: Better Teachers, Better Schools* (San Francisco: Jossey-Bass, 1992), along with Roger Soder, John I. Goodlad, and Timothy J. McMannon (eds.), *Developing Democratic Character in the Young*, and Stephen John Goodlad (ed.), *The Last Best Hope: A Democracy Reader* (both San Francisco: Jossey-Bass, 2001). See also John Goodlad and Timothy J. McMannon (eds.), *The Public Purpose of Education and Schooling* (San Francisco: Jossey-Bass, 1997), and Roger Soder (ed.), *Democracy, Education, and the Schools* (San Francisco: Jossey-Bass, 1996).

66. Lerner, *Revolutions Revisited*, p. 43.

67. Raymond Aron, *Main Currents in Sociological Thought*, trans. Richard Howard and Helen Weaver (New York: Doubleday, 1968), 1:257, 274.

Chapter Five

1. Thomas Cleary (ed. and trans.), *Zen Lessons: The Art of Leadership* (Boston: Shambhala, 1989), p. 98.

2. Donald W. Hendon, *Classic Failures in Product Marketing: Marketing Principles Violations and How to Avoid Them* (Lincolnwood, Ill.: NTC Business Books, 1992). See also Robert F. Hartley, *Bullseyes and Blunders: Stories of Business Success Failure* (New York: Wiley, 1987), and Robert F. Hartley, *Management Mistakes and Successes*, 3rd ed. (New York: Wiley, 1992).

3. Not all things that fall apart can be put back together with such frankness and forthrightness. For example, at the time of this writing, Firestone Tire Company is in considerable trouble over recalls and lawsuits, and there is reasonable speculation that the tire brand will have difficulty time recovering.

4. Peter Hall, *Great Planning Disasters* (Berkeley: University of California Press, 1982).

5. Edward Tenner, *Why Things Bite Back: Technology and the Revenge of the Unintended Consequences* (New York: Knopf, 1996), p. 98.

6. Harry Kemelman, *Monday the Rabbi Took Off* (New York: Fawcett Crest, 1972), p. 50.

7. See Lester J. Cappon (ed.), *The Adams-Jefferson Letters* (1959; Chapel Hill: University of North Carolina Press, 1987).

8. Thomas Powers, "Can Friendship Survive Success?" *Ms.* 3 (Jan. 1975): 16–18.

9. Marcel Mauss, *The Gift: Forms and Functions of Exchange in Archaic Societies*, trans. Ian Cunnison (New York: Norton, 1967), p. 80.

10. Cormac McCarthy, *The Crossing* (New York: Knopf, 1994), p. 193.

11. Lord Chesterfield, *Letters, Sentences, and Maxims* (London: Chesterfield Society, 1910), p. 330.

12. Euripides, *Orestes*, 507, trans. William Arrowsmith, in David Grene and Richmond Lattimore (eds.), *The Complete Greek Tragedies* (Chicago: University of Chicago Press, 1999), 4:222.

13. The out-of-sight, out-of-mind, firing approach to such problems is similar to what Philip Slater refers to as the "toilet syndrome" in *The Pursuit of Loneliness* (Boston: Beacon Press, 1970), pp. 15–18.

14. Or, with Ronald Laing, Montresor may be "hunting a hare whose tracks are in the mind of the hunters." See Laing, *The Politics of the Family* (New York: Vintage Books, 1972), p. 44.

15. Francis Bacon, "On Revenge," in *The Essays* (New York: Penguin Books, 1985), p. 72.

16. Ariel Dorfman, *Death and the Maiden* (London: Nick Hern Books, 1991).

17. See Mischa Glenny, *The Rebirth of History: Eastern Europe in the Age of Democracy* (London: Penguin Books, 1990), pp. 118–141, as well as Glenny, *The Fall of Yugoslavia: The Third Balkan War* (New York: Penguin Books, 1992). For a contrary view, see Susan L. Woodward, *Balkan Tragedy: Chaos and Dissolution After the Cold War* (Washington, D.C.: Brookings Institution, 1995).

18. Robert Wiebe, *The Segmented Society* (New York: Oxford University Press, 1975), p. 29.

19. Wiebe, *The Segmented Society*, p. 34.

20. Wiebe, *The Segmented Society*, p. 41.

21. Samuel Johnson, *The Rambler*, No. 60, Oct. 13, 1750, in Katharine Rogers (ed.), *The Selected Writings of Samuel Johnson* (New York: Signet, 1981), p. 62.

22. Mancur Olson, *Power and Prosperity: Outgrowing Communist and Capitalist Dictatorships* (New York: Basic Books, 2000).

23. Mark Twain, *Adventures of Huckleberry Finn* (Boston: Houghton Mifflin, 1958), p. 194.

24. Aristotle, *Ethics*, 1149a25, trans. J.A.K. Thompson (New York: Penguin Books, 1976).

25. Joseph Conrad, *The End of the Tether* (New York: Penguin Books, 1975), p. 92.

26. Fyodor Dostoevsky, *Notes from Underground*, trans. Richard Pevear and Larissa Volokhonsky (New York: Knopf, 1993); William Barrett, *Irrational Man: A Study in Existential Philosophy* (Garden City, N.Y.: Doubleday, 1958), p. 123. See also Joseph Frank, *Dostoevsky: The Stir of Liberation, 1860–1865* (Princeton, N.J.: Princeton University Press, 1986), Chap. 21.

27. John Lukacs, *The Duel: 10 May–31 July 1940, The Eighty-Day Struggle Between Churchill and Hitler* (New York: Ticknor & Fields, 1991), pp. 156–157.

28. W. T. Stead (ed.), *Last Will and Testament of Cecil John Rhodes* (London: "Review of Reviews" Office, 1902), p. 190.

29. Francis Bacon, "Of Envy," in *The Essays*, pp. 84–85.

30. Charles Siebert, "Sentenced to Nature," *New York Times Magazine*, Dec. 17, 2000, p. 60.

31. Thomas Hobbes, *Leviathan*, I, 8, ed. C. B. Macpherson (New York: Penguin Books, 1968), p. 140.

32. John Dickinson, *Letters from a Farmer in Pennsylvania* (Englewood Cliffs, N.J.: Prentice-Hall, 1962), p. 19.

33. Abraham Lincoln to Charles D. Drake and Others, Oct. 5, 1863, in Don E. Fehrenbacher (ed.), *Speeches and Writings* (New York: Library of America, 1989), 2:523.

34. Twain, *Adventures of Huckleberry Finn*, pp. 92–93.

35. Barbara Tuchman, *The March of Folly: From Troy to Vietnam* (New York: Knopf, 1984), p. 5.

36. Dorfman, *Death and the Maiden*, p. 59.

37. Timothy Garton Ash, "The Truth About Dictatorship," *New York Review of Books*, Feb. 19, 1998, p. 35.

38. On the extensive literature, see Desmond Tutu, *No Future Without Forgiveness* (New York: Doubleday, 1999), as well as Antjie Krog, *Country of My Skull: Guilt, Sorrow, and the Limits of Forgiveness in the New South Africa* (New York: Three Rivers, 2000). For reconciliation in Africa more generally, see Wolf Soyinka, *The Burden of Memory: The Muse of Forgiveness* (New York: Oxford University Press, 1999).

39. David A. Crocker, "Retribution and Reconciliation," Institute for Philosophy and Public Policy, University of Maryland [www.puaf.umd.edu/IPPP/Winter-Spring00]. For additional comments on Tutu's position, see Michael Ignatieff, *The Warrior's Honor: Ethnic War and the Modern Conscience* (New York: HarperCollins, 1998), pp. 169–178.

40. David A. Crocker, "Transitional Justice and International Civil Society: Toward a Normative Framework," *Constellations* 5 (Dec. 1998): 496.

41. David A. Crocker, "Civil Society and Transitional Justice," in Robert K. Fullinwider (ed.), *Civil Society, Democracy, and Civic Renewal* (Lanham, Md.: Rowman & Littlefield, 1999), pp. 380–381.

42. John Paul Lederach, *Building Peace: Sustainable Reconciliation in Divided Societies* (Washington, D.C.: United States Institute of Peace, 1997), p. ix.

43. Lederach, *Building Peace*, pp. 24, 26, 29.

44. "Discomfited Japan: Saying Sorry to the 'Comfort Women' Would Be Good for Japan, as Well as for Those It Mistreated So Terribly in Its 20th Century Wars," *Economist*, Dec. 16, 2000, p. 24. See also Yoshiaki Yoshimi, *Comfort Women: Sexual Slavery in the Japanese Military*, trans. Suzanne O'Brien (New York: Columbia University Press, 2000).

45. Susan Jacoby, *Wild Justice: The Evolution of Revenge* (New York: Harper & Row, 1983), p. 361.

46. Ignatieff, *The Warrior's Honor*, p. 188. See also R. Scott Appleby, *The Ambivalence of the Sacred: Religion, Violence, and Reconciliation* (Lanham, Md.: Rowman & Littlefield, 2000), especially Chap. 3.

47. Ignatieff, *The Warrior's Honor*, pp. 189–190.

48. Bacon, "On Revenge," p. 72.

49. William Faulkner, *Requiem for a Nun* (New York: New American Library, 1954), p. 229.

50. Cappon (ed.), *The Adams-Jefferson Letters*, pp. 275–285, 290; John A. Schutz and Douglass Adair (eds.), *The Spur of Fame: Dialogues of John Adams and Benjamin Rush, 1805-1813* (San Marino, Calif.: Huntington Library, 1966), pp. 156–160. See also L. H. Butterfield, "The Dream of Benjamin Rush: The Reconciliation of John Adams and Thomas Jefferson," *Yale Review* 40 (1950–1951): 297–319.

51. Eric Lomax, *The Railway Man: A POW's Searing Account of War, Brutality and Forgiveness* (New York: Norton, 1995), pp. 241, 269, 275.

52. Gesine Schwan, "Political Consequences of Silenced Guilt," *Constellations* 5 (Dec. 1998): 489.

53. Thomas Mann, *The Confessions of Felix Krull, Confidence Man* (New York: Vintage Books, 1969), p. 10.

54. Thomas Cleary (ed. and trans.), *The Book of Leadership and Strategy: Lessons from the Chinese Masters* (Boston: Shambhala, 1992), p. 51.

55. Fyodor Dostoevsky, *The Brothers Karamazov*, trans. Richard Pevear and Larissa Volokhonsky (San Francisco: North Point, 1990), Part I, Book 2, Chap. 2, p. 44.

56. Michael Ignatieff, *The Needs of Strangers: An Essay on Privacy, Solidarity, and the Politics of Being Human* (New York: Penguin Books, 1986), p. 11.

57. Blaise Pascal, *Pensées*, trans. A. J. Krailsheimer (New York: Penguin Books, 1966), p. 240.

58. Cleary, *Zen Lessons*, p. 84.

59. Schwan, "Political Consequences of Silenced Guilt," pp. 472–473.

Chapter Six

1. My examination of the elements of leadership in Philoctetes owes much to James Boyd White's wonderful analysis of the play "Heracles' Bow: Persuasion and Community in Sophocles' *Philoctetes*," *in Heracles' Bow: Essays on the Rhetoric and the Poetics of the Law* (Madison: University of Wisconsin Press, 1985), pp. 3–27.

2. Note, as with the discussion in Chapter Two, how the seeking of information by the Furies—"What place are you talking about?"—provides at the same time the information that they are becoming ready to reach some sort of reconciliation.

3. Aeschylus, *The Eumenides,* in David Grene and Richmond Lattimore (eds.), *The Complete Greek Tragedies,* trans. Richmond Lattimore (Chicago: University of Chicago Press, 1958), 1.812, 890–894. For a useful discussion of the role of the Furies and their reintegration, see William Barrett, *Irrational Man* (New York: Doubleday, 1956), Chap. 11.

4. Stewart W. Holmes and Chimyo Horioka, *Zen Art for Meditation* (Rutland, Vt.: Charles Tuttle, 1973), p. 34. For further examples of the emphasis on relationships in the ancient East, see Thomas Cleary's translation of the Taoist Huainanzi, in *The Book of Leadership and Strategy: Lessons of the Chinese Masters* (Boston: Shambhala, 1992) and Cleary's translation of selections of records and letters from the tenth- to thirteenth-century Song dynasty, in *Zen Lessons: The Art of Leadership* (Boston: Shambhala, 1989).

5. As does Odysseus at the end of Philoctetes. For a contemporary example of cutting off relationships and thus vanishing, we can, I would argue, consult the conclusion of *The Godfather, Part II,* with Michael Corleone sitting by himself. Everyone is gone. Michael himself is gone, or at least gone into himself, with only flashbacks, memories of his family during earlier, happier times.

6. Fyodor Dostoevsky, *The Brothers Karamazov,* trans. Richard Pevear and Larissa Volokhonsky (San Francisco: North Point, 1990), Part III, Book 7, Chap. 3. For a useful discussion of the relationship

between Aloysha and Grushenka in this chapter, see Nathan Rosen, "Style and Structure in *The Brothers Karamazov*," in *The Brothers Karamazov* (New York: Norton, 1976), pp. 841–861.

7. See C. P. Snow, *Variety of Men* (New York: Scribner, 1967), pp. 150–151, on Churchill, his expectations, and helping people rise above themselves.

8. White, "Heracles' Bow," p. 20.

9. On the distinctions between instrumental ends of education and education as a good in itself, see John I. Goodlad, *In Praise of Education* (New York: Teachers College Press, 1997), along with Neil Postman, *The End of Education* (New York: Knopf, 1995).

10. Herodotus, *Persian Wars*, III, 38 (New York: Modern Library, 1942), p. 229.

11. Eric Hoffer, *The True Believer* (New York: Harper & Row, 1951), p. 28. Similarly, see Chapter Two, note 47, of this book for Tocqueville's comments on the dangers of initiating change.

12. John Milton, *Paradise Lost*, 4.120–123 (New York: Odyssey Press, 1962), p. 87.

13. See, for example, Amitai Etzioni, *The Active Society: A Theory of Societal and Political Processes* (New York: Free Press, 1968), pp. 617–666.

14. For example, on mobility and administrative turnover in schools and colleges of education, see John I. Goodlad, *Teachers for Our Nation's Schools* (San Francisco: Jossey-Bass, 1990), pp. 126–132.

15. Abraham Lincoln, "Address to the Young Men's Lyceum of Springfield, Illinois: The Perpetuation of Our Political Institutions," in Don E. Fehrenbacher (ed.), *Speeches and Writings* (New York: Library of America, 1989), 1:28–36. For commentary on this speech, see Harry V. Jaffa, *Crisis of the House Divided: An Interpretation of the Issues in the Lincoln-Douglas Debates* (New York: Doubleday, 1959), especially Chap. 9.

16. Blaise Pascal, *Pensées*, trans. A. J. Krailsheimer (New York: Penguin Books, 1966), p. 67.

17. Tacitus, *The Annals,* trans. Michael Grant (New York: Penguin Books, 1977), p. 35.

18. Alexander Hamilton, The Federalist No. 72, in Garry Wills (ed.), *The Federalist Papers by Alexander Hamilton, James Madison, and John Jay* (New York: Bantam Books, 1982), p. 366.

19. Alan Palmer, *Alexander I: Tsar of War and Peace* (London: Weidenfeld and Nicolson, 1974), p. 282.

20. William Shakespeare, *Macbeth,* 1.3.123–125 (London: Methuen, 1986).

21. *Tao Te Ching,* No. 63, in *The Essential Tao,* trans. Thomas Cleary (San Francisco: HarperCollins, 1993), p. 48.

22. William Blake, "Jerusalem," Chap. 3, Plate 55, in David V. Erdman (ed.), *The Complete Poetry and Prose of William Blake,* rev. ed. (Berkeley: University of California Press, 1982), p. 205.

23. Holmes and Horioka, *Zen Art for Meditation,* p. 22.

24. Joseph Frank, *Dostoevsky: The Stir of Liberation, 1860–1865* (Princeton, N.J.: Princeton University Press, 1986), p. 333.

25. Thomas Hobbes, *Leviathan,* ed. C. B. Macpherson, (New York: Penguin Books, 1968), Part I, Chap. 10, p. 152.

26. Anthony Powell, *Books Do Furnish a Room,* vol. 10 of *A Dance to the Music of Time* (New York: Popular Library, 1986), pp. 144–145 (emphasis added).

27. Translated by Yasuko Horioka, in Holmes and Horioka, *Zen Art for Meditation,* p. 76.

Index